Property

Wolfgang Grassl

ACTON INSTITUTE

Christian Social Thought Series

Number 18 • Edited by Kevin Schmiesing

Christian Social Thought Series, Number 18

The Acton Institute acknowledges with gratitude the John Templeton Foundation for its support in the publication of this book.

All Scripture quotations are from the New American Standard Bible (NAS), unless otherwise indicated (e.g., NIV for New International Version).

Acton Institute
for the Study of Religion and Liberty

Cover image: Young Adults moving furniture and boxes from truck
Source: www.istock.com

ISSN 13: 978-1-938948-30-5

ACTONINSTITUTE

98 E. Fulton
Grand Rapids, Michigan 49503
Phone: 616.454.3080
Fax: 616.454.9454
www.acton.org

Printed in the United States of America

Contents

Foreword		*v*
I	The Essential Questions	1
II	Scripture on Property	9
III	Philosophers and Theologians on Property	19
IV	Economists on Property	33
V	The Church on Property	43
VI	A Christian View of Property	59
VII	Applications	73
References		89
About the Author		97

Foreword

"Essentially, Christianity is the same as communism." I was shocked the first time I heard that statement in conversation about the Catholic Church's social teaching, though I have heard and read many similar statements in the years since. My surprise stemmed from the fact that I knew well the arguments of *Rerum Novarum* and other papal encyclicals, where socialism is condemned in no uncertain terms. Claims about the compatibility of Christianity and communism contradict the centuries-long defense of private property that runs from Thomas Aquinas to Leo XIII, with many antecedents and heirs besides.

Yet such claims are not utterly without foundation. Those who study Scripture and the early Church know that Jesus urged the rich man to sell all he had, that some of the first Christians did hold property in common, and that the Church Fathers heaped much scorn on the acquisition of wealth. Those who study modern history know that, to put it mildly, the mind of the Church was not always in harmony with the liberalism that arose in Europe during the Enlightenment and that influenced current notions of property decisively. It is inaccurate, then, to say that the Church favors private property and to leave it at that.

The seemingly straightforward matter of private versus common property with respect to the Church's social tradition is therefore more complicated than it first appears. To appreciate it fully requires a knowledgeable analysis of Scripture, the Fathers, the Scholastic natural-law tradition, and, of course, modern Catholic social teaching. In the following pages, Professor Wolfgang Grassl provides just such an analysis. Recovering a genuinely Christian view of property requires extracting what is consistent with the gospel from the various ideologies that have grown up around and within Western civilization's political and cultural institutions over time. Professor Grassl performs this delicate surgery skillfully. Because our view of property lies at the foundation of so many practical issues and policy questions—a selection of which the author briefly highlights in the closing sections of this book—it is imperative that we consider carefully the wisdom contained in the Church's teaching on this subject. This teaching shows the path to a more just and genuinely prosperous society.

Kevin Schmiesing
Acton Institute

1 The Essential Questions

Few issues are as central to Christian social thought, and indeed to Western civilization, as is property. What is mine and what is thine, when we can legitimately regard it as such, and how we can protect our claims are issues that are as old as humankind. Already in the Hebrew Scriptures, property played an important role in the bonds among the Jews and in their individual and collective relationships to God. Property was considered to be a divine reward within revelation. Greek philosophers changed the emphasis by reflecting on the nature and justification of property, and Roman authors and statesmen cast them into law. The well-developed Roman law on property has become the basis of jurisprudence, legislation, and jurisdiction worldwide.

Property is crucial for an understanding of the human person. Where the Latin *proprietas* originally only meant "nature" or "quality," it later also came to mean "possession." However, the meaning of a special character (as a loan translation of the Greek *idioma*) has been dominant, and at its root is *proprium* (Greek *idion*) as an adjective meaning "one's own" or "peculiar to itself." The adjective is itself derived from *pro privo*, meaning "for the person." Different from objects, the properties of which are their characteristics, persons have not only intrinsic properties such as a particular height, eye color, or character, but also extrinsic (and alienable) property. However the legal status of property may be understood, persons have always some number of possessions over which they objectively have or over which they at least subjectively claim exclusive use. Property has therefore often been regarded as a cultural universal.[1] As an institution, it somehow belongs to being human although attitudes toward it may change.

Property has been understood either as part of human nature or as a social institution.[2] Philosophers and social scientists have been split on the issue, and their positions have been aligned along the nature-nurture divide. In his *Discourse on the Origin of Inequality* (1754), the French Enlightenment philosopher Jean-Jacques Rousseau famously argued that property was not a natural but a cultural and artificial institution that put an end to a blissful state of natural communism.[3] The original claim to real property was the beginning of evil, which Rousseau identified with civil society. Although he acknowledged the sanctity of the institution of property and that government should be created to protect it, property nonetheless established divisions in the natural world from which all further inequality followed. Karl Marx and Friedrich Engels were so fascinated with this idea of "original appropriation" that they saw the entire history of capitalism unfold from it. Consequently, in the *Communist Manifesto* (1848), they wrote that "the theory of the Communists may be summed up

---

1 See Donald Brown, *Human Universals* (Philadelphia: Temple University Press, 1991).

2 One of the most readable overviews of social thought with many references to property is Robert Nisbet, *The Social Philosophers: Community and Conflict in Western Thought* (New York: Thomas Y. Crowell, 1973). Specifically on property, see Richard Pipes, *Property and Freedom* (New York: Alfred A. Knopf, 1999).

3 Jean-Jacques Rousseau, *Discourse on the Origin of Inequality* (New York: Empire Books, 2012), pt. 2, 35.

in the single sentence: Abolition of private property."[4] Much of social science (and especially cultural anthropology) has followed Rousseau's lead in regarding property as a social creation that may then be regulated by the political will. The contrary position has been taken by those who see property as an ingredient of human nature. Historians have indeed shown that the idea of a "golden age" of communal ownership may be found in epic poetry but not in human history.[5] For Christians, this history starts with Adam's fall, which pushed humans into what Marx called the "realm of necessity." The fall damaged all relationships and upset the natural balance of the garden of Eden; it created scarcity and made property necessary (Gen. 3), but the recognition of property as an anthropological given also allows for different forms of social institutions.

Attitudes toward property have always reflected the type of society in which people lived. In 1857, the US Supreme Court found in the case of *Dred Scott v. Sandford* that slave owners had constitutionally protected property rights in their slaves. In South Africa today, traditional practices such as dowry payments to all intents still make women men's property. In recent years, some European countries have given animals a special legal status, which means that humans have limited property rights over them. Furthermore, because wealth entails the possession of property whereas ownership occurs at all levels of wealth, attitudes toward wealth and property will overlap but not be identical. For a long time, property was essentially land and buildings, then herds of husbandable animals, then precious metals, and only later consumables. The social institution of property has coevolved with theories about it. What can be property? How much importance is given to the acquisition of real or of personal property? What

---

4 Karl Marx and Friedrich Engels, *Manifesto of the Communist Party*, trans. Samuel Moore (Chicago: Charles H. Kerr, 1906), 34.

5 For an overview, see Pipes, *Property and Freedom*, chap. 2.

is the relationship between public and private property? Should the inheritance of property be taxed so as to create incentives for every generation to build up its own stock of property? Should a distinction be drawn between property in capital goods and in consumer goods? Is property restricted to tangible assets? How much control should people have over their property? Does property imply other rights or duties? May the state infringe on the property rights of individuals? Can there be freedom without private property? Answers to these and other questions reflect not only the social and legal thinking of societies but also their attitudes to the relationship between man and God. They indeed reveal a theology of property.

A particular attitude toward property has been fundamental to Western civilization, which has its roots in Jerusalem, Athens, and Rome.[6] However, property played various roles in Hebrew, Greek, and Roman thought. Whereas Hebrew culture prized material wealth, classical and Christian cultures either held it in contempt or preached indifference. The Hebrew Scriptures defined the place Yahweh attributed to humans, and the question of what was God's or man's was in the foreground. Property was under an eschatological mortgage, as centered on keeping the Mosaic Law, with manifold effects for the life of the Jewish people. The Greeks invented the City, and the rule of law was deemed to be a constitutive element for any good life in it. No longer was the line drawn between what was God's and man's but between what was mine and thine. Questions about property were found to be bound up with a universal human nature. Yet public reason, and the interests of the City, still prevailed over merely private concerns, as Plato, Aristotle, and the Stoics saw property under a social mortgage.

---

6 See Rémi Brague, *Eccentric Culture. A Theory of Western Civilization* (South Bend, IN: St. Augustine's Press, 2002); Philippe Nemo, *What Is the West?* trans. K. Casler (Pittsburgh: Duquesne University Press, 2006).

Only the Romans developed a comprehensive body of legal thought about property and codified it in private law. Different legal forms were distinguished: movable and real property, servitudes, easements, leases, usufruct, joint possession, heritable building rights, and so on. *Proprietas* was personal (and movable) property whereas *dominium* were the assets belonging to a household. Different from either form of property was mere control (*possessio*). However, according to the Code of Justinian, "ownership" and "legitimate use" cannot be permanently separated. For example, it is one thing for the owner of a book to let someone use it for a while. It is quite another matter to own the book and to grant someone *permanent* use of it or to agree not to recall it as long as the borrower wants to keep it. Pope John XXII in his bull *Ad conditorem* of 1322 pointed out that, from the point of view of Roman law, the latter case, for all intents and purposes, amounts to ownership. Only Roman law (but not the Germanic common law) had a concept of absolute ownership (*dominium*) as a characteristic of a free and self-directed citizen (*dominus*). Built on a particular understanding of the human person and his individual rights, Roman law was unmatched by previous civilizations as it emancipated property from any duty to society as such, apart from paying taxes. It became the basis of Western civilization with its belief in property as a human right under constraints of responsibility.

Yet the perception of a tension with Jerusalem lingers. In shifting the question of property to an allocation among humans, have we not overlooked the more fundamental divide between what is man's and what is God's? Can nature itself impose limits on what we can appropriate under the Law? How does the (Roman) law relate to the (Mosaic) Law? Can social convention be a foundation of a just order of property, as social contract theory would claim? Practically all current debates about property rely on explicit or implicit answers to these fundamental concerns. The civil and common law of the various nations have developed solutions, but they only barely disguise the fundamental truth that behind every political or legal question lies a great question of theology.[7]

The issues that are relevant today were already relevant for Abraham and his offspring. Even the forms by which property claims could be sustained—as the fruit of one's labor, as a gift from God, as the spoils of war, as an object of purchase or trade, as a piece of inheritance—are all found in Scripture and given different degrees of validation. Modern thinking about property not only stands on the shoulders of giants among human thinkers but is also founded on divine revelation. As with other central themes of social thought, such as labor, justice, peace, or commerce, the political and legal arrangements depend on philosophical positions that in turn are grounded in views about the relationship between God and man. Through the impact of Western thought on the legal orders of all nations, this long and rich tradition has come to frame property law throughout the world. Being cast in the form of constitutions, codes, and contracts, this legacy has long become universal.

At its heart lies an ethics of property that has developed within Christian thought. It straddles the fence between the belief that all human goods come from God and recognition of the autonomy given to man to pursue his own plans. To resolve this inevitable tension, scholastic authors resorted to ideas of natural law as first espoused by Stoicism and fitted these into the precepts of the Old and New Covenants. Property came to be seen as contributing to the common good, which was both an incentive and a limitation for private acquisition. The canon law of the Church was in many ways built on Roman law. It had little to say about personal property; its domain was and is humankind and its access to salvation through the community of the Church. It regulated ecclesiastical property, which the Church increasingly came to hold. Yet, the

---

7 See Juan Donoso Cortés, *Essays on Catholicism, Liberalism, and Socialism*, trans. W. McDonald (Dublin: M. H. Gill, 1879), bk. 1, chap. 1.

concept of ownership in canon law has a distinctively different meaning from that of secular law. For canon law, ecclesiastical ownership is rooted in the Church's understanding of its mission. Its inherent right to own property is of divine origin and can therefore not be abridged by secular law.[8]

Only indirectly, through its prohibition on usury, which was rooted in the Mosaic Law, did the Church affect the disposition of personal property. This norm, however, contradicts the liberal tradition of political thought into which many in the West would today want to insert their views on property.[9] The complexity of the teachings of the Church is borne out by Blessed John Paul II's statement that the right to private property "has always been defended by the Church up to our own day" whereas "at the same time, the Church teaches that the possession of material goods is not an absolute right, and that its limits are inscribed in its very nature as a human right."[10]

A full understanding of the many issues surrounding property that arise in any society today is therefore hardly possible without considering the legacy of Jerusalem, Athens, and Rome as synthesized and transmitted by Christian tradition. It is only natural that the Catholic Church, as the heir to scholastic thought and to Canon Law and as a defender of natural law, should play a major role in the debate about property. Within Christianity, Catholic social teaching (CST) has without doubt developed the most elaborate set of norms that touch on property as a divine gift,

---

8 See John Paul II, 1983 Code of Canon Law (*Codex iuris canonici*), cc. 1255f., 1259f.

9 See John J. Coughlin OFM, *Canon Law: A Comparative Study with Anglo-American Legal Theory* (Oxford: Oxford University Press, 2011), chap. 4.

10 John Paul II, *Centesimus Annus*, § 30.

social institution, and individual right.[11] For Catholics, magisterial teaching on property is not the private opinion of any pope or of the Curia but an integral part of the faith as applied to the understanding of man and his relations to God and the world.[12]

Many disciplines now study various aspects of property. These comprise history, anthropology, sociology, economics, philosophy, law, theology, political science, and business administration. In any single discipline such as economics, various directions and schools are concerned with issues of property.[13] The understanding of a multifaceted issue will increase when it is elucidated from several angles. A concise overview that seeks to outline a Christian position on property rooted in CST need not consider contributions of all of these disciplines. It needs to lay out the biblical evidence, the teachings of the Church, and the main views advocated by philosophers, theologians, and social thinkers as to the nature and justification of property. More importantly, it needs to show how a Christian position resolves conflicts over property that include some of the most debated issues in the spheres of society, politics, and law today. Not all of these issues can be mentioned in a brief text. Rather, a viewpoint in harmony with CST will be proposed that readers can use as a standard by which to judge currently disputed questions.

---

11 CST is here understood as the magisterial teaching of the Catholic Church as it has been expressed in encyclicals and other instruments of papal teaching and in authoritative documents such as the *Catechism of the Catholic Church* (Vatican City: Libreria Editrice Vaticana, 1997) and the *Compendium of the Social Doctrine of the Church* (Vatican City: Libreria Editrice Vaticana, 2004).

12 See John Paul II, *Centesimus Annus*, 1991, § 3 and Pius X's earlier *Singulari quadam* (1912), which impose on all Catholics "a sacred and inviolable duty, both in private and public life, to obey and firmly adhere to and fearlessly profess the principles of Christian truth enunciated by the teaching office of the Catholic Church" (*Singulari*, § 2).

13 See Enrico Colombatto, ed., *The Elgar Companion to the Economics of Property Rights* (Cheltenham, UK: Edward Elgar, 2004).

II Scripture on Property

According to Scripture, the ultimate origin and owner of all goods is God; only sin is due to man alone. All property belongs to God, and humans owe gratitude for the temporary right to use it, however much they may consider themselves proprietors. The Hebrew Scriptures valued material wealth as a sign of divine favor. Thus men such as Abraham, Isaac, Jacob, Solomon, and Job attained many possessions because of their faith. Abraham's servant proclaimed: "The Lord has greatly blessed my master, so that he has become rich; and He has given him flocks and herds, and silver and gold, and servants and maids, and camels and donkeys" (Gen. 24:35). In all cases, property was a divine gift (Gen. 26:12–14; 30:27, 30; 33:11; 2 Chron. 1:1; Job 42:10–17; Ps. 8:8; Sir. 11:10–28 RSV). Property had no stronger title than that of a temporary loan from God who was the source and ultimate owner even of the works of human hands. The Ten Commandments stated that the Israelites were not to steal nor even to covet another's property (Ex. 20:2–17; Deut. 5:6–21). Mosaic Law protected personal property and even placed a psychological cause of its disturbance under sanction. Solomon was not covetous because he did not ask God for wealth, possessions, or honor but instead for knowledge and wisdom to govern his people. This is why Solomon was given both and made rich beyond comparison (2 Chron. 1:7–12). In fact, fifteen different commandments in the

Pentateuch guarantee property rights by outlawing acts such as using inaccurate scales and weights (Deut. 25:13), robbing (Lev. 19:13), withholding wages (Lev. 19:13), or not returning the lost property of others (Deut. 22:3). In other books, the dilution of currency, in essence inflation, is presented as a transgression against property (Isa. 1:22; Ezek. 22:18–22).

Ownership of property was not considered as sinful nor was its absence given any moral value. The Hebrew Scriptures legitimize real and movable property if it is lawfully acquired: "Spend the money for whatever your heart desires: for oxen, or sheep, or wine, or strong drink, or whatever your heart desires" (Deut. 14:26). Yet wealth always implied an obligation to assist the poor and needy and to be honest in business dealings. The prophets did not chide the wealthy for having excessive property; they were rebuked when they failed to make good use of it (Ezek. 16:49; Isa. 58:7; Jer. 22:16). Together with the widows and the aliens, the poor were under God's special protection (Isa. 61:1). The prophet Amos gave a stern warning to those "at ease in Zion" (Amos 6:1) who "trample the needy, to do away with the humble of the land" (Amos 8:4) that the "day of calamity" would come (Amos 6:3). Isaiah and Micah uttered similar warnings (Isa. 5:8; Mic. 2:2). The Hebrews were forbidden to reap right to the edges of the field or to gather up fruit and ears that had been forgotten or had fallen on the ground because they belonged to the poor (Lev. 19:9–10; 23:22; Deut. 24:19–22). Acquisition of property also incurred the risk of idolatry, including worshiping a false deity. Only those owners who maintained the proper rank of values were truly blessed—property was first to serve the Lord; then the poor; widows; aliens; and, finally, the community. Whoever kept this order could, as a residual claimant, use God's bounty for his family and himself.[1]

---

1 See Pontifical Council for Justice and Peace, *Towards a Better Distribution of Land: The Challenge of Agrarian Reform* (Vatican City: Libreria Editrice Vatacana, 1997), § 24.

David asked God to disclose the purpose of making an offering to him who, after all, was the creator and owner of the entire universe (1 Chron. 29:14–17). This clearly rhetorical question points to an important characteristic of property in the Hebrew Scriptures: It has a purpose. The Promised Land was given to the twelve tribes as an "inheritance" (Josh. 13:33; 18:7; Deut. 10:9; 18:1–2), with the priestly tribe of Levi receiving a different allotment. If abundance of property comes from an abundance of divine blessing, failure to utilize the property according to God's intentions soon leads to loss or perdition. The Israelites were accountable for the use to which they put God's gifts. This is exemplifed in the celebration of the capable wife who not only "considers a field and buys it ... [and] senses that her gain is good" but also "extends her hand to the poor, and ... stretches out her hands to the needy" (Prov. 31:16–20). For all types of property, God commanded its use for the needy, and, for one particular type of property, he laid down even more specific rules.

In the Hebrew Scriptures, the character of personal (or movable) property was distinct from that of real property. Not only were the Jews guided from exile into the Promised Land as the fulfillment of their covenant with God, the Law of Moses intended that land could not be owned indefinitely: "The land, moreover, shall not be sold permanently, for the land is Mine; for you are but aliens and sojourners with Me" (Lev. 25:23). The Hebrews were fully aware of this restriction, for at a later date the psalmist wrote: "The earth is the Lord's, and all it contains" (Ps. 24:1). The divine prerogative to land was safeguarded by the institution of the Jubilee year. Every fifty years, sold land was to automatically revert to the original owner of the patrimony. Selling land therefore amounted to no more than a loan until the onset of the next Jubilee year, and the price was to be calculated accordingly (Lev. 25:13–17). Even before that event, the seller had the right to redeem the land from the buyer if he could afford to do so; if he could not, his next of kin could substitute. As far as we know, a

Jubilee year was never actually celebrated. This part of the Mosaic Law was intended to stabilize the socioeconomic structure of ancient Israel by reducing the mobility of real property. Property received from God as inheritance was not freely transferable (Ezek. 45:1; 1 Kings 21:3).[2] No similar restrictions were placed on the ownership or transfer of movable property.

However, in the ninth and eighth centuries before Christ, kings donated land to officials, and small farmers ran up debt and mortgaged their land and themselves. Transactions in real property, including the rejection of its alienation, are thus found throughout the Hebrew Scriptures. In the monarchical period, Naboth refused to sell his vineyard to King Ahab (1 Kings 21:3), Abraham purchased a field and the cave of Machpelah from Ephron (Gen. 23), and Jacob bought land from the sons of Hamor (Gen. 33:19–20). The legal procedure for such transactions in pre-exilic Judah is also set forth in the Old Testament (Jer. 32:6–16). The five daughters of Zelophehad, who lived during the Exodus from Egypt, raised before Moses the case of a woman's right and obligation to inherit landed property in the absence of a male heir in the family (Num. 26:33; 27:3; Josh. 17:3). Next of kin had a right of preemption, which limited free transfer and placed property law into the interest of tribal structures. Ownership of land involved obligations. Thus Abimelech insists that Abraham as an immigrant to Gerar respect the land (Gen. 21:23). In fact, the land itself has rights to lie fallow during the sabbath rest, to revert to its original owner during the Jubilee, and more. In all this, different ideologies or régimes of land use among the Israelites can be distinguished. The emphasis in the Old Testament was placed on land as the source of wealth, as a conditional grant from God, as family inheritance, or as a host country—these functions not being mutually exclusive.

---

2 See also Norman C. Habel, *The Land Is Mine: Six Biblical Land Ideologies* (Minneapolis: Fortress Press, 1995), chap. 4.

The prophets Isaiah, Micah, and Amos bemoaned the increasing alienation of what God had meant to be a permanent allocation of land among the tribes of Israel (Isa. 5:8; Mic. 2:1–2; Amos 2:6; 5:11). Priestly reformers attempted to counteract it by prohibiting interest (Ex. 22:25), commanding that land lie fallow in the seventh year (Ex. 23:10), and declaring a Jubilee year (Lev. 25). Disposition of property came under rules that benefited the community.

The clear insistence on divine ownership limits any overly generous reading of the command given to humans to "subdue" the earth and to establish "rule" over it (Gen. 1:28). Humans were thereby given a job description rather than free reign over God's earth, for their actions were placed under a divinely sanctioned regimen. Human freedom to exploit creation was immediately qualified by dietary restrictions (Gen. 1:29), which were lifted in part only after the flood. Property, particularly in land, was always held derivatively, temporarily, and by grace rather than desert or achievement. Not only will "those who wait for the Lord ... inherit the land," but especially the humble, those blessed by him, and the righteous (Ps. 37:9, 11, 22, 29). God proclaimed that transgression of the Law would result in banishment from the land. In rather drastic terms, he commanded: "You are therefore to keep all My statutes and all My ordinances and do them, so that the land to which I am bringing you to live will not spew you out" (Lev. 20:22). Essential to the Jewish understanding of property is God's ultimate (and often quite direct) agency. Attempts to derive from the creation story the right of humans to exploit the "fruits of the earth" according to their whim amount to a regrettable misconstrual of the biblical evidence. Hebrew Scripture is clear about a duty of protection: "You shall not defile the land in which you live, in the midst of which I dwell; for I the Lord am dwelling in the midst of the sons of Israel" (Num. 35:34). Wisdom literature, in particular, emphasizes that property, as such, does not have ethical relevance—only its use. The wise man knows its proper place in life and does not mistake a means for an end: "Do not set your heart on your wealth" (Sir. 5:1 RSV) is therefore sound advice.

The Greek Scriptures retain the emphasis on the purpose of property, but they no longer privilege land and simply take ownership, purchase, and transfer of goods including real estate for granted (Matt. 13:34–35; Acts 4:34–37). Persons have the right to dispose of their property as they wish (Matt. 20:15). Yet, in keeping with Mosaic Law, Christ makes it clear that property must be used for the benefit of those in need (Matt. 5:42). It thus has to serve the weaker members of the community even though this was not always the highest priority (Mark 14:5–7). Where the Old Testament saw property under an eschatological mortgage, the New Testament sees it under a social mortgage as it requires responsible use under the command of charity. Property was now given a deeper ethical status. Ownership as such is not condemned, but excessive wealth may bring about spiritual decay: "Truly I say to you, it is hard for a rich man to enter the kingdom of heaven. Again I say to you, it is easier for a camel to go through the eye of a needle, than for a rich man to enter the kingdom of God" (Matt. 19:23–24; similar versions in Mark 10:24–25 and Luke 18:24–25). The Gospels nowhere romanticize poverty, but they show that material possessions are not related to righteousness and justification before God. The rich man sees Lazarus, whom he had scorned while Lazarus was begging at his door, in Abraham's bosom in paradise while he himself was confined to the torments of hell (Luke 16:19–31). Excessive wealth is a burden, and may be an impediment to salvation if good use is not made of it: "You cannot serve God and wealth" (Matt. 6:24). Following the Hebrew Scriptures, there is a strong warning that property tends to foster idolatry and moral corruption. This is why poverty should be embraced: It gets the priorities right and does not detract from service to the Lord. The first of the Beatitudes reads: "Blessed are you who are poor, for yours is the kingdom of

God" (Luke 6:20). Jesus did not condemn material possessions or wealth as an evil per se, but he repeatedly referred to it as a hindrance to full commitment to God (Mark 4:19; Matt. 13:22; Luke 8:14). Concentration on property on this earth conjures up an illusion of wealth where there may be spiritual poverty, for true riches can only be hoped for in heaven. Nowhere is this point made clearer than in the Sermon on the Mount (Matt. 6:19–21; Luke 12:33–34). Furthermore, as the story of the repentant tax collector Zacchaeus shows, true discipleship requires the right use of earthly riches.

Thus the New Testament takes a complex (if in no way ambiguous) view of property.[3] Following the Hebrew Scriptures, all property belongs to God and can only be received by grace: "Give us this day our daily bread" (Matt. 6:11). Yet, in his incarnate form, "the Son of Man has nowhere to lay His head" (Matt. 8:20). On the one hand, as an ingredient of wealth, property must be avoided because materialism presents a danger to salvation (Luke 8:14). The story of the rich man does not claim wealth, as such, to be an obstacle. Instead, the unwillingness to give up wealth in order to follow Jesus (Mark 10:17–31; Matt. 19:16–29; Luke 18:18–30) is the obstacle. Even though property is allowed, it may not always be salvific and prudent to focus on its acquisition and enjoyment. On the other hand, the theme of the Hebrew Scriptures that prosperity is a blessing from God, who promised to regale the Jews if they would follow his commandments (Gen. 12:2), has dimmed. Because of the positive Hebrew attitude toward property, the disciples were "astonished" at Jesus' advice to the rich man to abandon his possessions (Mark 10:26). More characteristically, Paul tells the faithful of Philippi that God will provide for their needs, but he does not promise them property (Phil. 4:19).

---

3 David Murchie, "The New Testament View of Wealth Accumulation," *Journal of the Evangelical Theological Society* 21, no. 4 (1978): 335–44.

Biblical exegesis has insisted that in the plan for salvation, material wealth must never be more than a means toward a transcendent end. Under both the old and the new covenants, the faithful are cautioned not to fall into idolatry by seeking property as an end: "Those who want to get rich fall into temptation and a snare and many foolish and harmful desires which plunge men into ruin and destruction" (1 Tim. 6:9). This is why "the love of money is a root of all sorts of evil" (1 Tim. 6:10)—it establishes wrong priorities and detracts from the true order of goods: "Do not store up for yourselves treasures on earth, where moth and rust destroy, and where thieves break in and steal. But store up for yourselves treasures in heaven, where neither moth nor rust destroys, and where thieves do not break in or steal; for where your treasure is, there your heart will be also" (Matt. 6:19–21). Paul counsels those who purchase something to treat it "as though they did not possess" (1 Cor. 7:30)—no property is theirs to keep.

As a mere means, however, property is morally neutral. In the earliest Christian communities described in the Acts of the Apostles, there were those who practiced almsgiving and generosity to the poor (Acts 9:36; 10:2–4) and those who gave priority to worldly property over the needs of others (Acts 5:1–11, 8:14–24). Most characteristically, these communities were described as follows: "All those who had believed were together and had all things in common; and they began selling their property and possessions and were sharing them with all, as anyone might have need" (Acts 2:44–45). The prophetic voice of James, the Lord's brother and presumably the first bishop of Jerusalem, came down upon those who transgressed (as in the tradition of Isaiah, Ezekiel, Jeremiah, Micah, and Amos), and he condemned the oppressive rich as standing before God's imminent judgment (James 1:10–11; 5:1–6). The somewhat milder voice of the apostle John reminded them to get their priorities right: "Do not love the world nor the things in the world. If anyone loves the world, the love of the Father is not in him" (1 John 2:15). In analogy to the well-known distinction between a positive and negative concept of freedom, one may account for the biblical evidence by distinguishing between a positive and negative idea of property.[4] Property gives both the power to do good for others and may yet (as a privation of good) detract from the true purpose of life.

What is not morally neutral is the use of property, which depends on the human soul. Because property is but a gift, having received larger gifts requires greater willingness to repay God by sharing with others:

> Last year you were the first not only to give but also to have the desire to do so. Now finish the work, so that your eager willingness to do it may be matched by your completion of it, according to your means. For if the willingness is there, the gift is acceptable according to what one has, not according to what one does not have (2 Cor. 8:10–12 NIV).

Christians are judged for their use of property by the attitude they have toward it, which should be joyful, grateful, and mindful of its role as a means toward following Christ.

Means are judged by their use toward an end: "You will know them by their fruits" (Matt. 7:16). Once property serves the welfare of others, it must also do so well. In the parable of the talents, those slaves were rewarded who had made the best use of their master's property (Matt. 25:14–30; Luke 19:12–28). Property may be used to increase income—provided it is done by the law of love for God and neighbor. Just as the two slaves applied prudence in investing what was entrusted to them, good stewardship requires making responsible use of property that is ultimately God's alone. *Stewardship*, then, epitomizes the biblical teaching on property.

---

4 See Isaiah Berlin, "Two Concepts of Liberty," in *Four Essays on Liberty* (London: Oxford University Press, 1969).

III Philosophers and Theologians on Property

Philosophers have mainly been interested in whether property (like other institutions such as justice or marriage) was instituted by nature (*physis*) or rather by human convention and law (*nomos*). Those who believed in property as part of human nature tended to have a more accommodating view of it, while those who regarded it as merely a social arrangement tended to have a more dismissive view. The second area of interest to philosophers has been the individual or collective nature of property and the respective merits of the two types of ownership. For Christian theology, the debate between nature and convention became one about the origin of property in God alone or in a human sphere that is at least somewhat autonomous. Property as a social fact also raised the question of its purpose—to satisfy private desires or to serve the needs of others—and thus of its proper use.

Greek philosophers were not of one opinion on property. Plato showed disdain for it (and for any kind of materialist attitude) when in the ideal city of the *Republic*. He forbade property ownership for the guardians while conceding private property to the lowest class, including the farmers who would provide the guardians' food. Together with property, he eliminated family relationships and all other forms of privacy from his totalitarian and collectivist model. Collective ownership was necessary to promote the pursuit of the common interest and to avoid the social divisiveness that results from private endeavors.[1]

Several schools of philosophy such as the Cynics and Stoics followed Plato's lead. Cicero and Seneca told the story of a Greek philosopher who, having lost his family and all worldly possessions to war, proclaimed that he carried all his belongings with him—justice, virtue, and prudence.[2] The Stoics made the point that true property was immaterial and consisted of one's virtues and reputation. Cicero emphasized that private property was not established by nature because it was originally common. It becomes private either through long occupancy, conquest, or by due process of law.[3] The early church fathers took a similar position when they emphasized the divine origin of property and supported the sharing of worldly goods.[4] Aurelius Ambrosius, better known as Saint Ambrose, bishop of Milan and one of the four great doctors of the Western church, expressed a view representative of the time when he proclaimed that "nature has poured forth all things for all men for common use," elaborating on it as follows: "God has ordered all things to be produced so that there should be food in common for all, and that the earth should be the common possession of all. Nature, therefore, has produced a common right [*jus commune*] for all, but greed has made it a private right [*jus privatum*]."[5] Saint Basil the Great, the Bishop of Caesarea, and Saint Gregory of Nyssa concurred that property

1 See Plato, *The Republic*, bk. 5, 462b–c.

2 Cicero, *Paradoxa Stoicorum*, I.1.8; Seneca, *Epistulae Morales ad Lucilium*, bk. 1, letter 9, 18–19.

3 Cicero, *De Officiis*, bk. 1, chap. 7, 21.

4 See Charles Avila, *Ownership: Early Christian Teaching* (Maryknoll: Orbis Books, 1983).

5 Aurelius Ambrose, *De Officiis Ministrorum* [Duties of the Clergy], bk. 1, chap. 132; see also Louis J. Swift, "*Iustitia* and *Ius Privatum*: Ambrose on Private Property," *American Journal of Philology* 100, no. 1 (1979): 176–87.

was only justified by its use for others; Basil therefore rejected a natural right of inheritance. Private property was largely seen as the result of original and individual sin and, if not by itself evil, at least it was a treacherous institution. Born into an affluent family, Saint Basil gave away all his possessions to the poor and needy. Saint John Chrysostom preached against the abuse of wealth and personal property. Saint Clement of Alexandria demanded that all property not needed by one's own family be given to the poor. By and large, the church fathers showed skepticism toward private property and even more so toward its accumulation. It could be justified neither by natural nor by divine law, which the churchmen tended to equate.[6]

Implicit in this position is the idea of positive community—all mankind owned the earth equally—rather than negative community—all of mankind owned none of the earth and possession originated in occupation. Because dominion means exclusive control over an object, and bringing something into being is the criterion for possessing natural dominion over it, only God can have natural dominion over the world. The command to populate the earth (Gen. 1:28) can at most give indirect and derived powers to humans but does not establish their property rights. These remain conditional and are at best justified by their proper use.[7]

Plato's stance against property, often transmitted by the Stoics, remained influential. In the Renaissance period, Thomas More and Tommaso Campanella, in describing their utopian societies, did away with private property. In the Enlightenment period, Jean-Jacques Rousseau deplored the existence of property as

---

6 Jacob Viner, *Religious Thought and Economic Society*, ed. J. Melitz and D. Winch (Durham: Duke University Press, 1978), chap. 1.

7 The separation between conditional *dominium*, which was derived from God's unrestricted dominion over the universe and presumed property was the topic of theological debates throughout the Middle Ages. See Christopher A. Franks, *He Became Poor: The Poverty of Christ and Aquinas' Economic Teachings* (Grand Rapids: Eerdmans, 2009).

such, which he regarded as a social institution that arose from the dissolution of a blissful original state of nature. In the nineteenth century, the French anarchist politician and philosopher Pierre-Joseph Proudhon in his posthumously published *Theory of Property* (1863–1864) argued that "property is theft," "property is impossible," "property is despotism," and "property is freedom." His argument for theft inspired Karl Marx to develop his theory of surplus value, according to which the value created by workers in excess of their own labor cost was appropriated by the capitalist as gross profit. For both Proudhon and Marx, property in means of production establishes permanent despotism over workers. In asserting that property is freedom, Proudhon referred not only to the product of an individual's labor, but to the peasant's or artisan's home and tools of trade and to the income he received by selling his goods. For Proudhon, the only legitimate source of property is labor. What one produces is one's property and anything beyond that is not.

There has thus been a tradition that despised private property and accepted it only if it was held in common. It originated with Plato and by way of Rousseau would continue to the modern experiments with communism. This philosophical lineage was opposed by a liberal tradition whose representatives defended private property for a number of reasons.

Plato's disciple Aristotle held a more positive view. For him, private ownership is grounded in nature: "Property of this sort then seems to be bestowed by nature upon all."[8] It promotes virtues such as prudence and responsibility, whereas "that which is common to the greatest number has the least care bestowed upon it."[9] Property ownership creates positive incentives: "When everyone has a distinct interest, men will not complain of one another, and they will make more progress, because every one

8 Aristotle, *Politics*, bk. 1, chap. 3, 1256b.

9 Aristotle, *Politics*, bk. 2, chap. 1, 1261b.

will be attending to his own business."[10] Yet, Aristotle saw the purpose of property in making a good life possible for a household (*oikonomía*). Accumulation beyond a household's needs was unworthy of a free man, for it would detract him from worthier pursuits such as the cultivation of friendships or philosophy.[11] Aristotle disdained maximization of wealth. Thus, traders were held in contempt as were the artisans (*banausoi*) who accumulated property through the work of their hands. Aristotle saw a necessary relationship between property and freedom. To be free (and thus eligible for citizenship rather than confined to slavery) was to belong to oneself, and this was connected with having sufficient distance from one's desires to enable the practice of virtuous self-control. Truly free men enjoy leisure because of having property and by not valuing the accumulation of more. Overall, Aristotle saw three possible property arrangements: (1) private ownership but common use, (2) common ownership but private use, and (3) common ownership and common use.

Private ownership and private use would be immoral and detrimental to the communitarian nature of the *polis*. Option 2 would defraud the *polis* whereas option 3 would deprive citizens of their right to property. Aristotle therefore advocated option 1: "It is better for possessions to be privately owned, but to make them common property in use."[12] In essence, this prefigured the teaching of the Church.

Saint Augustine of Hippo took a similarly accommodating view when pointing out that the wealth of Abraham did not preclude his entry into paradise and that it was only its use that defined the morality of property. Augustine respected the secular laws on property and inheritance. This position was clearly opposed to the postulate sustained by Pelagians and other heretical sects

---

10 Aristotle, *Politics*, bk. 2, chap. 2, 1263a.

11 Aristotle, *Politics*, bk. 1, chap. 3, 1256a–1257b; bk. 7, chap. 1, 1323b.

12 Aristotle, *Politics*, bk. 2, chap. 2, 1263a–b.

that claimed the impossibility for any wealthy person to attain salvation or, for that matter, retain membership in the Church. While not following these zealots in their experiments with communism, the Fathers were concerned about those who, like Lazarus in Christ's parable (Luke 16:19–31), had no property and yet possessed equal dignity (and sometimes greater faith). Even though private property was seen as lawful, it was so only conditionally.[13]

The rediscovery of Aristotle during the Middle Ages helped to shift the debate away from the relative merits of private or communal property to the proper purpose of personal ownership within a Christian concept of the human person. The origin of property in God entails the proper purpose and use of worldly goods—a principle that would later be called the universal destination of goods.[14] Saint Thomas Aquinas was the first to give it a clear expression. He followed Aristotle in claiming that individual property has positive effects by bringing about a more careful procurement, better management, and more peaceful allocation of goods. However, in regard to their use, created things are subject to man by reason of his intellect and will: Man is able to use material things for his own profit and to provide for his needs. It is in this sense that man has dominion over other creatures and may transform parts of creation according to his own plans.[15]

---

[13] See Richard J. Dougherty, "Catholicism and the Economy: Augustine and Aquinas on Property Ownership," *Journal of Markets & Morality* 6, no. 2 (2003): 479–95.

[14] *Catechism of the Catholic Church* (Vatican City: Libreria Editrice Vaticana, 1997), § 2402; Albino Barrera, OP, *Modern Catholic Social Documents and Political Economy* (Washington, DC: Georgetown University Press, 2001), chap. 10; Manfred Spieker, "The Universal Destination of Goods: The Ethics of Property in the Theory of a Christian Society," *Journal of Markets & Morality* 8, no. 2 (2005): 333–54.

[15] Aquinas, *Summa Theologica*, II-II, q. 66, a. 1.

Aquinas thus legitimized private property for instrumental reasons. However, he did not regard it as natural but "as a result of human agreement, which belongs to the positive law."[16] There is nothing about any piece of land that according to nature would make it belong to any one more than any other because God gave the world to all men. Therefore, no one can claim any exclusive right to any material good by nature.[17] The appropriation and division of things is instead based on human law, and their use must be communitarian: "Man ought to possess external things, not as his own, but as common, so that, to wit, he is ready to communicate them to others in their need."[18] The desire for possessions can even be unlawful if property is sought as an ultimate end; with too great solicitude; or if one must fear that by following conscience one will lack necessities.[19] Because human law is subordinate to the natural (or moral) law, the Church teaches that in cases of obvious and urgent need, the taking of necessities such as food or clothing does not amount to theft.[20] While the right to private property is thus not something inherent in the nature of man or of creation, neither is it unnatural. It is not contrary to the law of nature that one should make use of material goods for one's own benefit. In fact, Aquinas tells us that positive law (i.e., the law of the land) must include a dispensation for private property. If all things were held in common, then there would be great disorder because, as Aristotle had already realized, what is common to all is often cared for by none. Moreover, private property also helps

---

16 Aquinas, *Summa Theologica*, II-II, q. 6, a. 2: *secundum humanum condictum, quod pertinet ad ius positivum.*

17 Aquinas, *Summa Theologica*, II-II, q. 57, a. 3.

18 Aquinas, *Summa Theologica*, II-II, q. 66, a. 2.

19 Aquinas, *Summa Theologica*, II-II, q. 55, a. 6.

20 Aquinas, *Summa Theologica*, II-II, q. 66, a. 7; see Paul VI *Gaudium et Spes*, § 69; John XXIII, *Mater et Magistra*, § 43; *Catechism of the Catholic Church*, § 2408.

to curb greed, for each is given an incentive to maintain what is one's own, and each is discouraged from taking what is another's.[21] The Spanish late scholastics (such as Francisco de Vitoria and Juan de Mariana) built on these ideas when they pointed out that private property ensures peace and justice.[22] The Jesuit theologian Francisco Suárez included property among the natural rights that, as an institution, no government could lawfully abolish even though individual pieces might be confiscated. Yet, never must the accumulation of wealth become the goal of life—on this all churchmen were agreed.[23] With this realistic and commonsense position on property, a standard had been developed that CST has largely followed until today.

Although it was foreshadowed by philosophers such as Aristotle, the liberal tradition has its true roots in seventeenth-century individualism: "Its possessive quality is found in its conception of the individual as essentially the proprietor of his own person or capacities, owing nothing to society for them."[24] The historically most influential position was elaborated by John Locke. He saw the preservation of property as the reason why humanity has assembled into states in the first place.[25] Property enjoys historical and therefore legal priority: the political order does not introduce it as Thomas Hobbes thought, but private property requires an effective government for its protection. Locke argued that, as a

---

21 Aquinas, *Summa Theologica*, II-II, q. 66, a. 2.

22 See Leonard P. Liggio and Alejandro A. Chafuen, "Cultural and Religious Foundations of Private Property," in *The Elgar Companion to the Economics of Property Rights*, ed. Enrico Colombatto (Cheltenham, UK: Edward Elgar, 2004), 3–7.

23 See Amintore Fanfani, *Catholicism, Protestantism, and Capitalism* (Norfolk: IHS Press), chap. 5.

24 C. B. Macpherson, *The Political Theory of Possessive Individualism: Hobbes to Locke* (Oxford: Oxford University Press, 1962), 3.

25 John Locke, *The Second Treatise on Civil Government* (Amherst, NY: Prometheus, 1986), chap. 9, sec. 124.

natural right, "every man has a 'property' in his own 'person.' This nobody has a right to but himself."[26] This axiom of self-ownership was at odds with the Christian view of man as dependent on God. Although God has not divided up the earth, reason shows that private property is in accordance with God's will. The title to such property is found in labor. Individuals earn property rights by mixing their own labor with unowned resources. Underlying this argument is the homestead principle according to which something can be appropriated by putting an unowned resource to active use, which for Locke was again a natural right. Defenders of absolute property rights typically trace their reasoning to Locke, although they often overlook that the philosopher also recognized a limit to property wherein man can no longer use what has been appropriated from nature through work. With Locke, the objective foundation of property in revelation, nature, reason, or the moral law that was characteristic of the Aristotelian tradition up to late scholasticism and to Hugo Grotius gave way to the subjective account that was to dominate the Modern Age. It also ignored any social duties that property entails.

David Hume shared in the subjective approach but rejected any such natural right as the title to property. The multiple possible origins of property—as "any possession acquired by occupation, by industry, by prescription, by inheritance, by contract, etc."—cannot all have been instructed by nature.[27] Rather, property is a social institution, a "convention enter'd into by all the members of the society to bestow stability on the possession of those external goods, and leave every one in the peaceable enjoyment of what he may acquire by his fortune and industry."[28] Private property is

---

[26] Locke, *The Second Treatise on Civil Government*, chap. 5, sec. 26, 20.

[27] David Hume, *An Enquiry Concerning the Principles of Morals* (La Salle, IL: Open Court, 1966), sec. 3, pt. 2, 35.

[28] David Hume, *A Treatise of Human Nature* (Oxford: Oxford University Press, 2007), bk. 3, sec. 2.2, 314.

justified by its social utility, as is justice itself, of which property is a consequence: "Our property is nothing but those goods, whose constant possession is established by the laws of society; that is, by the laws of justice.... The origin of justice explains that of property. The same artifice gives rise to both."[29] In fact, Hume seemed to believe that property was the only object of justice. Arguing from the same tradition, Immanuel Kant even posited property rights as an axiom in arguing that stealing was contradictory. To allow stealing would be tantamount to abolishing property, which, in turn, would render theft impossible. The legal order of a state prevents this implication.

Representatives of the liberal (including what, in the American parlance, is called the libertarian) tradition have thus been split on whether property was instituted by nature or by convention. They agree on understanding humans as individuals who are free of social obligations and therefore on rights to acquire, use, and dispose of property limited only by human law. Those who believe in natural law (or, not identically, a set of natural rights) hold that property is guaranteed by it and thus comes before any man-made law, which only serves to protect it. They also reject any relational obligation or other limitation of an absolute title, leaving charitable use to owners' individual choice. The philosopher Robert Nozick argued that every individual has an absolute right to whatever assets he or she lawfully acquires. Imposing extra taxes on very affluent persons, for example through a graduated or progressive income tax, then amounts to nothing less than theft and to an infringement of fundamental rights.[30] Other philosophers in the liberal tradition, by following Hume rather than Locke, reject natural rights and see property as due to a social contract or convention. In John Searle's social ontology,

---

29 Hume, *A Treatise of Human Nature*, 315.

30 See Robert Nozick, *Anarchy, State and Utopia* (New York: Basic Books, 1974), chap. 7.

property is an institutional fact that is brought into being by the assignation of a particular status to things. Land is then made property not by (unopposed) enclosure, as Locke would have it, or by mere fiat, which would raise problems of legitimacy, but rather by agreement.[31]

Conservative thinkers have tended to share with Hume an emphasis on the social utility of property. As defenders of the Old Régime in society, politics, and morality, they have seen it as a stabilizing force. Thus, the French counterrevolutionary philosopher and statesman Louis de Bonald advocated broad ownership of land as the true well-spring of devotion to the common good. Landed property is an expression of the rootedness of families in a particular region for which they bear responsibility.[32] This argument would later be continued by writers such as G. K. Chesterton and Hilaire Belloc in the distributist tradition of Catholic thought. Chesterton goes even further: Property commits its owner to productive use. Just like sex, it must not be reduced to its enjoyment but be seen as "participation in a great creative process."[33] It is for this reason that the means of

---

[31] See Errol Meidinger, "Property Law for Development Policy and Institutional Theory: Problems of Structure, Choice, and Change," in *The Mystery of Capital and the Construction of Social* Reality, ed. Barry Smith, David M. Mark, and Isaac Ehrlich (Chicago: Open Court, 2008), 229–60 and other essays in this volume. A mere convention of course may appear to be a weak title by which a specific claim can be protected. It remains unclear whether it can also explain intellectual property rights, which pertain not to things at all but only to their use or reproduction. They are brought into being by legislation rather than private agreement though both legislation and contracts may count as social conventions.

[32] See Louis de Bonald, *The True and Only Wealth of Nations: Essays on Family, Society, and Economy*, trans. Christopher Blum (Ave Maria, FL: Sapientia Press, 2006).

[33] G. K. Chesterton, "The Well and the Shallows," in *The Collected Works of G. K. Chesterton*, vol. 3 (1935; repr., San Francisco: Ignatius Press, 1990), 502.

production should be spread as broadly as possible rather than be centralized under the control of the state, a few large businesses, or wealthy individuals.

Theologians have taken a more positive or a more negative view on property, but overall they have shunned clear identification with either the liberal or the conservative line. Some have transitioned between views. Reinhold Niebuhr, the American theologian from the German Reformed tradition, began by recommending in 1931 the abridgment of "absolute property rights" and their replacement with tax-financed social insurance. He saw at the time an identity between the ideals of Christianity and socialism. By 1935 he regarded property rights held by small traders and farmers as giving them a chance to perform a social function.[34] Niebuhr, however, came to oppose the Social Gospel movement, which was a Protestant body of thought aiming at social reform. Whereas the various Protestant churches have often engaged in social activism, some Protestant theologians have freely admitted that their own tradition has never developed a theologically unified body of social teaching and, consequently, no theory of property.[35]

Modern philosophy has gone beyond a uniform treatment of property by recognizing that how artifacts, animals, houses, and ideas are owned is different.[36] Even under the perspective of ontology, real estate has different characteristics from other forms of property.[37] Jurisprudence has now replaced philosophy (and, for that matter, economics) as the discipline that deals most fruit-

---

34 See Reinhold Niebuhr, *An Interpretation of Christian Ethics* (New York: Harper & Brothers, 1935), chap. 6.

35 See Stephen J. Grabill, "Protestant Social Thought," *Journal of Markets & Morality* 12, no. 1 (2009): 1–3.

36 See Philip Pettit, "Freedom in the Market," *Politics, Philosophy and Economics* 5, no. 2 (2006): 131–49.

37 See Heiner Stuckenschmidt, Erik Stubkjaer, and Christoph Schlieder, eds., *The Ontology and Modelling of Real Estate Transactions* (Aldershot: Ashgate, 2003).

fully with issues of property. Although legal thinking and codes of law always reflect social trends, and jurisprudence by necessity relies on philosophical (and one might add: theological) positions, property law has developed into a highly technical subject apparently far removed from issues of nature versus convention or individual versus community. Yet, when the most influential (and most widely exported) civil laws of modern times—the French Code Napoléon and the German Bürgerliche Gesetzbuch—were written, they were built on the codification of Roman law. By dividing law into the law of persons, property, and acquisition of property, the Napoleonic Code followed the division of Roman civil law into sections on persons, things, and actions. Property itself has a tripartite definition as the right to possess, use, and dispose of a thing. These philosophical distinctions reflect Aristotle's philosophy as received by Rome. The very fact that property in the Roman law belongs to private law (*ius privatum*), as concerning a relationship between persons, has set the stage for many centuries of legal thinking and practice. Similarly, the common law of property as developed by judges rather than as statutes reflects, as in the feudal origin of a property title in fee simple (the most common form of private property ownership), the legal and political thinking of a society. Under both legal régimes, institutions of property continue to evolve, presenting new challenges for ethical evaluation.

IV Economists on Property

Because scarcity is an ineradicable characteristic of the human condition, all societies have developed rules for determining legitimate entitlement to desired objects. Economists generally take for granted that everything of value—both tangible and intangible goods—has an owner. Exceptions are made for common-property resources such as air and international waters. For a long time, property was therefore not regarded as a topic for serious economic consideration.[1] In 1890, the preeminent textbook still remarked that "the rights of property, as such, have not been venerated by those master minds who have built up economic science."[2] This changed only during the twentieth century. Specific systems of property rights were now subjected to economic analysis. These included worker cooperatives and slavery as well as common-property resources, such as radio frequencies, public goods, club goods, and licenses and franchises. In a complementary fashion, historians paid attention to different forms of holding economic

1 See, for example, Joseph A. Schumpeter, *History of Economic Analysis* (New York: Oxford University Press, 1954), which in the course of some 1,200 pages makes barely a reference to property as a basic category in the history of economic thought.

2 Alfred Marshall, *Principles of Economics*, 8th ed. (London: Macmillan, 1920), 40.

goods over history and across cultures. One of the findings derived from these investigations is that civilization does not by necessity require private property, although economic development may.[3] Another finding is that seemingly all civilizations have given a special role to land as the primordial source of sustenance.

Property, as such, does not play a major role in the classical and neoclassical schools of thought, which simply assumed it but developed few arguments in its defense. Other schools such as the physiocrats, Marxists, or institutionalists developed more reflection on property. For physiocratic authors such as Richard Cantillon, property ownership defined an entire social class whose interest in a static society based on land rent was different from the new dynamic class of entrepreneurs. Even Adam Smith still saw land as a special type of property characterized by its greater scarcity. Property was not an important topic for him, but his account of "previous" (or "original") accumulation inspired Marx's theory of class distinctions between possessors and nonpossessors. Smith reduced property to "the property which every man has in his own labour"[4] and regarded civil government as necessary for its protection. It is "in reality instituted for the defense of the rich against the poor, or of those who have some property against those who have none at all."[5] As a result of the industrial revolution, property as means of production other than land increased and caused a shift of interest toward capital goods. By modern times, the question of property, which had long focused on its social origin and responsibility, has been reduced to one about rights. The French economist Frédéric Bastiat defined the liberal

---

3 See Ludwig von Mises, *Human Action*, 4th ed. (San Francisco: Fox & Wilkes, 1996), chap. 15, sec. 3, 264.

4 Adam Smith, *An Inquiry into the Nature and Causes of the Wealth of Nations* (Oxford: Oxford University Press, 1976), bk. 1, x.c., 12.

5 Smith, *An Inquiry into the Nature and Causes of the Wealth of Nations*, bk. 5, i.b., 3.

position by making property constitutive of liberty and restricting government to the function of safeguarding the life, liberty, and property of individuals.

In the twentieth century particularly, the neoinstitutionalist school has advanced the discussion on property. Ronald Coase argued that without transaction costs it is economically irrelevant as to whom initial property rights are assigned; the problem of externalities will be solved by agreement based on efficiency alone. Property-rights allocation will hence matter only in determining distribution, not efficiency. With sufficient transaction costs, however, initial property rights will have a nontrivial effect. They should then be assigned such that the owner of the rights wants to take the economically efficient action.[6]

This Coase theorem has found applications in policy making and jurisdiction. One normative conclusion is that government should create institutions that minimize transaction costs, so as to allow misallocations of resources to be corrected as cheaply as possible. From a Catholic viewpoint, concerns have been raised about distributional consequences and particularly about the compatibility of an efficiency solution based on low-transaction costs with an equity solution based on preference for the poor.[7]

Other economists have built on these findings and have presented property rights as the most efficient tool for internalizing negative and positive externalities. These are effects from which others, but not their producers, either suffer or benefit. The concentration of both the benefits and costs of an economic action on owners rather than outsiders creates incentives to utilize

---

6 See Ronald H. Coase, "The Problem of Social Cost," *Journal of Law and Economics* 3 (1960): 1–44.

7 See Robert T. Miller, "The Coase Theorem and the Preferential Option for the Poor," *Journal of Catholic Social Thought* 5 (2008): 65–80.

resources more efficiently.[8] Real property typically generates most external effects on neighbors and thus suggests private ownership. Yet, there are also common-property resources such as a local artisanal culture where shared trademarks and quality standards are successfully managed as club goods from the consumption of which members can be excluded.[9]

Thus, modern economics thinks of property in terms of property rights. It is envisaged as a bundle of such rights. Not only are these the rights to possess, use, manage, consume or destroy, modify, transmit and alienate, but they are also the rights to the income from property, to its use as forfeit or collateral, and so forth.[10] Economics has developed a consensus view on these that is challenged only on the margins. Property rights are the prerequisite for exchange. They thus make the price system possible, and they provide individuals not only with incentives to create wealth but also with insurance against risk, thus facilitating economic growth. Because individuals cannot trade what they do not own, property rights are foundational for market exchange, which, in turn, implies market prices. Friedrich von Hayek has argued that without the price system the information that markets provide about how resources should be used could not be discovered. Unless property rights are secure, individuals cannot employ their resources productively.

Some economists have added that property rights solve the problem of commons. In a famous article, Garrett Hardin argued that a "tragedy of the commons" occurs when there is no

---

8 See Harold Demsetz, "Toward a Theory of Property Rights," *American Economic Review* 57, no. 2 (1967): 347–59.

9 See Tiziana Cuccia and Walter Santagata, "Collective Property Rights for Economic Development: The Case of the Ceramics Cultural District in Caltagirone, Sicily," in *The Elgar Companion to the Economics of Property Rights*, ed. Enrico Colombatto (Cheltenham, UK: Edward Elgar, 2004), 473–88.

10 See Lawrence C. Becker, *Property Rights: Philosophic Foundations* (London: Routledge, 1977).

means to exclude others from a communally used resource. Under these conditions, the resource will be overused to the point of destruction so long as each user gains more benefits than the costs he bears. In Hardin's example, villagers shared access to a common field. Each could put as many cattle on the field as he desired because no one had the right to exclude another. As a result, each villager added cattle so long as the last cow added benefited him more than it cost him. Since a portion of the cost created by the additional cow was the reduction in grass available to the cows owned by others, no villager took into account the total cost to the village of the additional cows. Unsurprisingly in Hardin's example, the field ended up with so many cattle grazing on it that it was overgrazed and destroyed. All the villagers were worse off, yet no one had an incentive to stop the overgrazing.[11] This outcome could be prevented by either more government regulation or by privatizing the commons so that the owner can charge a price that reflects the increasing utilization or depletion of the resource. Economists in the liberal tradition have clearly favored a solution of common-resource problems (overfishing of the oceans, air pollution, vandalism in parks, highway congestion, and so forth) through transfer into private property.[12] Opponents often object that an efficient pricing solution can be imposed by government even in the absence of private property. Though the allocation of fair shares may be technically possible, advocates of free markets have retorted that it would still harbor a fundamental conflict between the ideal of a just distribution and that of personal liberty.[13]

---

[11] See Garrett J. Hardin, "The Tragedy of the Commons," *Science* 162, no. 3859 (1968): 1243–48.

[12] See Mises, *Human Action*, chap. 23, sec. 6.

[13] See Milton Friedman and Rose Friedman, *Free to Choose* (San Diego: Harcourt, 1980), chap. 5; James M. Buchanan, "Property as a Guarantor of Liberty," in *Property Rights and the Limits of Democracy*, ed. Charles K. Rowley (Cambridge: Cambridge University Press, 1993).

Catholic social teaching has long prioritized concerns for a clean and safe natural environment. Economists, scientists, and politicians have developed plans for implementation, particularly from a Christian motivation. The sustainability of projects affecting the environment has become important, not least because of a moral obligation to future generations.[14] In fact, papal teaching has appropriated economic arguments, not least that an internalization of environmental externalities (under intergenerational equity) is needed to achieve the most efficient use of natural resources.[15] Catholic theologians and economists have remained skeptical, however, with regard to a "tragedy of the commons." Too easily may it be misused to justify morally reprehensible "solutions" for other alleged "commons" problems such as overpopulation.[16] In fact, Hardin himself advocated strict population control and voluntary euthanasia. Catholic social teaching emphasizes that scarcity of resources requires neither privatization nor stifling regulation but rather reveals "a *pressing moral need for renewed solidarity*."[17] Magisterial teaching here contradicts both interventionist and liberal economics.

According to the free-market view, a secure system of private property rights is an essential part of economic freedom. For some, "private ownership of the means of production is the fundamental institution of the market economy."[18] This system includes two main rights: to control and benefit from property and to transfer

[14] See John Paul II, *Centesimus Annus*, § 36; Benedict XVI, *Caritas in Veritate*, § 27, 48–51.

[15] Benedict XVI, *Caritas in Veritate*, § 50; see also Wolfgang Grassl and André Habisch, "Ethics and Economics: Towards a New Humanistic Synthesis for Business," *Journal of Business Ethics* 99, no. 1 (2011): 37–49.

[16] See J. Brian Benestad, *Church, State, and Society: An Introduction to Catholic Social Doctrine* (Washington, DC: Catholic University of America Press, 2011), 353.

[17] Benedict XVI, *Caritas in Veritate*, § 49.

[18] Mises, *Human Action*, chap. 24, sec. 4, 682.

property by voluntary means. These rights offer people the possibility of autonomy and self-determination according to their personal values and goals. Property rights are seen as basic human rights, as indeed CST claims. Economists also impute to property a more utilitarian value: secure property rights reduce uncertainty and encourage investments, thus creating favorable conditions for an economy to be successful.[19] Empirical evidence suggests that countries with strong property-rights systems have economic growth rates almost twice as high as those of countries with weak property rights and that a market system with significant private-property rights is an essential condition for democracy.[20] According to Hernando de Soto, much of the poverty in less developed countries is caused by the lack of Western-style systems of laws and well-defined property rights. De Soto argues that because of legal barriers, particularly the absence of land registration systems and appropriate documentation, poor people in those countries cannot utilize their assets to produce more wealth.[21] The Church, which has always had a keen awareness of social needs and political deficiencies, had already drawn attention to this fact.[22]

A similar argument can be made for intangible property. Where classical economists used to draw a sharp distinction between land and movable property, this categorical divide has increasingly weakened, not least because of the emergence of intellectual

---

19 See Bernard H. Siegan, *Property and Freedom: The Constitution, the Courts, and Land-Use Regulation* (Piscataway, NJ: Transaction Publishers, 1997).

20 See David L. Weimer, "The Political Economy of Property Rights," in *The Political Economy of Property Rights* (Cambridge: Cambridge University Press, 1997), 8.

21 See Hernando De Soto, *The Mystery of Capital* (New York: Basic Books, 2003).

22 Pontifical Council for Justice and Peace, *Towards a Better Distribution of Land* (Vatican City: Libreria Editrice Vaticana, 1997), § 14.

property as a third class of assets.[23] However, access to registration and legal protection of inventions are very unequal around the world. Many ideas produced in less developed countries therefore never gain international recognition while established companies in highly developed countries use their market power to extract economic rent from often questionable patents, trademarks, and copyrights. Economic analysis does not solve questions about property that are in the province of social ethics and politics. De Soto's work makes clear that the institution of property is essentially public—it would not exist without laws and their enforcement.

Catholic social thinkers have developed a property ethics that dispenses with the utilitarian assumptions that underlie mainstream economic reasoning. Instead of attempting to demonstrate the compatibility of extraneous economic assumptions (on scarcity, utility, property, and so forth) with CST, they have derived economic theory from CST itself.[24] Catholic economists had and have an economic doctrine but not an economic theory; their doctrine has never accepted the independence of theoretical from ethical propositions. Thus, the Jesuit Heinrich Pesch recognized a right to private property even though it cannot be unconditional and absolute but rather involves obligations. It is thus a subjective right directed at the well-being of the person, family, and society, which "establishes appropriate limits to the acquisition, expansion, and use of property."[25] Because of the clear position CST has held on the legitimacy of private property, as well as

---

23 See William M. Landes and Richard A. Posner, *The Economic Structure of Intellectual Property Law* (Cambridge, MA: Belknap Press, 2003).

24 See António Almodovar and Pedro Teixeira, "The Ascent and Decline of Catholic Economic Thought, 1830–1950s," *History of Political Economy* 40 (2008): 62–87.

25 Heinrich Pesch, SJ, *Ethics and the National Economy*, trans. Rupert Ederer (Norfolk: IHS Press, 2004), chap. 5, 75.

on the moral difference between ownership and use, Catholic economists have had only one major point of contention: What does the social mortgage on property mean in practice? Some tend to relegate it to individual charity by relying more on the moral autonomy of believers; others see this autonomy as very limited and favor forms of collective management of property. In many countries, the Church has sponsored cooperatives of farmers, artisans, shopkeepers, and consumers, and papal teaching has long supported this movement. Most recently, Benedict XVI issued a challenge to entrepreneurs and managers to develop new forms of enterprise that go beyond the dichotomous logic of capitalism. This includes overcoming the traditional division between private and public property, which no longer reflects the reality of a complex economy.[26] The challenge is to develop new juridical and fiscal structures, governance systems, and management practices that creatively transform both the traditional public and private sectors, rather than aim at a separate third sector. Neither private property nor profit are at the bottom of social ills, but they are both to be judged by whether they support "the goal of a more humane market and society." The pope hopes that bridging social dichotomies will also set free creative energies that lead to a better use of human and natural resources: "*The very plurality of institutional forms of business gives rise to a market which is not only more civilized but also more competitive.*"[27]

This program requires a reorientation of thinking about property. No longer is simple ownership decisive for prosperity, but, rather it is access to resources and the opportunities they provide. What is important is not *having* but *participating*. As markets have become transformed into networks, producers engage in

26 See Wolfgang Grassl, "Hybrid Forms of Business: The Logic of Gift in the Commercial World," *Journal of Business Ethics* 100, suppl. 1 (2011): 109–23.

27 Benedict XVI, *Caritas in Veritate*, § 46.

collaboration and consumers substitute lease or membership for purchase, property becomes a matter of access rather than mere title and control. By implication, the economics of property should not only be concerned with its production, as supporters of free markets would have it, but also with its distribution, as the social justice movement demands. The real challenge for Christians is to avoid seeing the economic process as a zero-sum game of win-or-lose but instead to create new opportunities for all to acquire property or access to its benefits, to use the state to support those who would otherwise fall into destitution, and, in doing so, to abide by the economic principles of incentives and rewards subject to the more fundamental law of charity.

V The Church on Property

The Christian Church developed its teaching on property on the grounds of biblical evidence, the writings of the church fathers and the scholastic theologians, and experiences of Christian communities. Two interpretations of biblical texts became particularly important: First, that prior to Adam's fall, personal property was unknown and second, that Christ and the apostles owned nothing either individually or in common. Consequently, individual property was seen as the consequence of original sin, and the early Christians, most of whom belonged to the lower classes of society, renounced ownership. The Acts of the Apostles describe their communities as follows: "For there was not a needy person among them, for all who were owners of land or houses would sell them and bring the proceeds of the sales and lay them at the apostles' feet, and they would be distributed to each as any had need" (Acts 4:34–35). The economic order of the early church was simple and radical.[1] In the generation after Christ's death, Christian communities pooled their property, and this form of organization prevailed until at least the age of Emperor Constantine. Throughout history, radical and utopian (and often heretical groups have drawn their inspiration from real or imagined

---

[1] David Murchie, "The New Testament View of Wealth Accumulation," *Journal of the Evangelical Theological Society* 21, no. 4 (1978): 342.

prelapsarian and pre-Constantinian property communism. This communitarian focus of early Christianity, however, was also a move away from following the original commandment of giving to anybody who might be in need.

As Christian communities after Constantine's time grew and became property owners, canons of law were developed that regulated the management and use of material goods. Pronouncements on personal property were typically separated from those on ecclesiastical property. Where the first was derived from certain autonomy and responsibility of the human person that no public order must undermine, the latter was guaranteed by the sacred nature of the Church, particularly by its necessary freedom from encroachment by any civil powers. The same rules about the just acquisition of property applied to singular persons and families as well as to the Church except where ecclesial entities (such as monasteries, religious orders, or the pope) were at the same time sovereign rulers.

Just as the doctrine of communal property developed from within the Church, so did the later doctrine of personal property. The gradual transition came about in the High and late Middle Ages. Once Christianity had expanded in Europe and a shifting balance between secular powers (*regnum*) and ecclesiastic power (*sacerdotium*) had evolved, the Church became interested in curtailing absolutist pretensions of worldly rulers. That property could legitimately be personal and did not automatically belong to the sovereign was a result of the Papal Revolution in the eleventh and twelfth centuries when the Western Church established its political and legal unity and its independence from emperors, kings, and feudal lords.[2] Indirectly, the recognition of private property rights benefited from the assertion of an ecclesiastic sphere that by divine law was autonomous and immune from civil encroachment

---

2 See Harold J. Berman, *Law and Revolution: The Formation of the Western Legal Tradition* (Cambridge: Harvard University Press, 1983).

even outside the political suzerainty of the Church. Theologians and canonists who defended the rights of the Church also won a battle for a civil order that protected personal property under law.

Even during this period, itinerant preachers and new religious orders lived as the "poor of Christ" (*pauperes Christi*) and renounced property for themselves and for their communities. Various heretical groups held to a dualistic opposition between an evil world and a desired kingdom of heaven, proclaimed the end time near, and rejected all property. The new mendicant orders were committed to living in poverty. The Spirituals, as the more radical wing of the Franciscans, demanded that the Church at all levels abandon property as the followers of Saint Francis had done. This would of course have weakened the position of the pope in his epic struggle with the emperor. When Innocent III in 1208 condemned the Waldensians, he demanded of them the abjuration of their belief that personal property was incompatible with salvation. In the fourteenth century, the question of whether Christ and the apostles had indeed renounced all property, led to intense fights between zealous Franciscan factions and the papacy, and similar opinions were prosecuted by the Inquisition.[3] In the fifteenth century, however, the Italian Franciscans pioneered the institution of pawnbrokers (*monti di pietà*) that were capitalized by the merchant class and, in an early form of organized charity, made loans to the poor that avoided usury.

Within the Church, from the High Middle Ages until the Catholic Reformation in the wake of the Council of Trent, two constituencies, scholastic philosopher-theologians and canon lawyers, advanced doctrine on property. Because nearly all in the small group of learned men at this time held clerical offices, even practitioners of civil law could be counted as working within the Church. Medieval canonists, in particular, championed private

---

3 See Christopher A. Franks, *He Became Poor: The Property of Christ and Aquinas' Economic Teachings* (Grand Rapids: Eerdmans, 2009), 56–61.

ownership, its unfettered if rightful acquisition, and its free disposition.[4] Pope Innocent IV insisted that even non-Christians could legitimately own property, for he regarded this right as an element of the natural law. Although this position found its opponents, the papal right to legislate over infidels was eventually sustained and with it the concession of property rights.[5]

Aquinas had emphasized the distinctiveness of the human person within the order of creation. From the creation of humans in God's image follows what Catholic social teaching (CST) would later call their inherent dignity: Every human being is a person of ultimate worth, to be treated always as an end and not as a means toward some end. This principle established itself slowly, however. The Church saw no problem with a high concentration of property (and a near-monopolization of real property outside cities) in the hands of large landowners. In many parts of Europe, the Church was itself one of the largest owners of estates and businesses, and the older religious orders counted as feudal lords over sovereign territories. By the end of the seventh century, the church owned a third of all land in Gaul, and, by the twelfth century, the Benedictine Abbey of Monte Cassino alone owned 2 duchies, 20 counties, 400 towns and villages, 250 fortresses, 336 granges, 23 harbors, and 1,662 churches.

During European colonization of territories in Africa, Asia, and America, the Church had no unanimous position on the legitimacy of slavery. Some popes opposed it, notably Pope Paul III, whose bull *Sublimus Dei* (1537) explicitly forbade the enslavement of the indigenous peoples of the Americas who were rational beings with souls and were thus entitled to liberty and property. In time, the view prevailed that because of their inalienable dignity, human beings could not be appropriable objects. In this spirit,

---

4 See James A. Brundage, *Medieval Canon Law* (London and New York: Longman, 1995), 79.

5 Brundage, *Medieval Canon Law*, 163.

the Jesuit Reductions in Paraguay (and later in Argentina and Brazil) between 1609 and 1767 gave 140,000 Tupí-Guaraní people freedom, yet without property, inheritance, or money. The Church recognized property as an individual right only much later.

It was during the nineteenth century that, as a response to the social question, CST was revived under the name of "social Catholicism." In Germany, the Bishop of Mainz, Wilhelm Emmanuel von Ketteler, rejected both capitalism and socialism. Inspired by Aquinas, he taught that God alone is the ultimate and absolute owner of all things, that man has only a restricted right to use these things, and that in using them he must always have regard for the order that God had established for the universe.[6] Catholic associations such as the Fribourg Union further developed this "third way" into a corporatism that sought to reclaim the medieval guild economy built around vocational groups of employers and employees. Property was a tool meant to bridge the class divide. The Catholic Church in Europe became associated with farmers, artisans, and shopkeepers who took pride in their productive capital and typically reduced personal consumption in order to develop their family businesses. The Church supported the formation of production and marketing cooperatives among business people and of trade unions among workers in order to strengthen economic independence, which was also seen as contributing to moral reform. The strong social activity of laity in the nineteenth and early twentieth century revived magisterial CST. At the same time, Christian (and in some countries specifically Catholic) political parties were formed and adopted this social agenda.

---

6 Wilhelm von Ketteler, *The Social Teachings of Wilhelm Emmanuel Ketteler, Bishop of Mainz* (Washington, DC: University Press of America, 1981), 12.

On the one hand, in *Rerum Novarum* (with which he inaugurated modern CST in 1891) Leo XIII opposed class struggle and condemned the socialist solution of communal property:[7]

> The right to possess private property is derived from nature, not from man; and the State has the right to control its use in the interests of the public good alone, but by no means to absorb it altogether. The State would therefore be unjust and cruel if under the name of taxation it were to deprive the private owner of more than is fair.

On the other hand, "*private ownership must be preserved inviolate.*"[8] With this strong advocacy of property, Leo XIII went beyond the traditional Thomistic position, which understood property as a derived right necessitated by imperfect human nature. Property may have a positive social function by providing incentives to deploy diligence and creativity. The pope also emphasized developing an ownership society that enabled even lower-paid workers to accumulate property gradually.[9]

However, the encyclical not only rejects the socialist design of abolishing private property but also the liberal understanding of property as implying an unfettered right to use or abuse it (*ius utendi et abutendi*). Not only is it critical of any strong concentration of capital, Leo XIII clearly expresses, with reference to Aquinas, that the use of property must be directed toward the common good. Once personal needs are met, individuals have a duty to give to others.[10] He then formulates an ethic of property that has lost nothing of its importance:[11]

7 Leo XIII, *Rerum Novarum*, § 47.

8 Leo XIII, *Rerum Novarum*, § 24.

9 Leo XIII, *Rerum Novarum*, §§ 5, 65.

10 Leo XIII, *Rerum Novarum*, § 22.

11 Leo XIII, *Rerum Novarum*, § 28.

> Christian morality, when adequately and completely practiced, leads of itself to temporal prosperity, for it merits the blessing of that God who is the source of all blessings; it powerfully restrains the greed of possession and the thirst for pleasure—twin plagues, which too often make a man who is void of self-restraint miserable in the midst of abundance; it makes men supply for the lack of means through economy, teaching them to be content with frugal living, and further, keeping them out of the reach of those vices which devour not small incomes merely, but large fortunes, and dissipate many a goodly inheritance.

Leo XIII thus combined the political question of a just property order with the moral question of how to manage temporal goods. His opposition to socialism was in part founded on its rejection of property accumulation by the working class. This idea was very progressive at the time and strongly influenced Catholic and conservative parties and trade-union movements particularly in Europe and Latin America.[12]

Pius XI in *Quadragesimo Anno* proclaimed private property to be essential for the development and freedom of the individual and that those who oppose it deny personal freedom and development.[13] The pope also emphasized that private property implies a social obligation. It loses its morality if it is not directed at and subordinated to the common good, which is understood as "the sum of those conditions of social life which allow social groups and their individual members relatively thorough and ready access to

---

12 See Oswald von Nell-Breuning, SJ, *Reorganization of Social Economy* (New York: Bruce Publishing Company, 1936); "The Formation of Private Property in the Hands of Workers," in *The Social Market Economy: Theory and Ethics of the Economic Order*, ed. Peter Koslowski (Berlin: Springer, 1998), 291–328.

13 Pius XI, *Quadragesimo Anno*, §§ 44–52.

their own fulfillment."[14] Therefore, governments have not only a right but indeed a duty to "bring private ownership into harmony with the needs of the common good,"[15] for example, by pursuing redistribution policies through taxation and welfare plans. In extreme cases, the state may even expropriate private property.[16]

Leo XIII ventured farthest into understanding property as part of the natural law, and subsequent papal teaching retreated from *Rerum Novarum* on this point. Pius XI, John XXIII, and all subsequent pontiffs explicitly dissociated themselves from a labor theory of property or value.[17] John XXIII placed the right of private ownership of goods including capital goods as "part of the natural order."[18] Yet, Paul VI explicitly rejected unrestricted private property.[19] John Paul II would later forcefully reiterate that private property is not an absolute value and finds its "complementary principle" in the universal destination of all goods.[20] Within a correct hierarchy of values, "being" always must trump "having" because humans are not defined by their material possessions, "especially when the 'having' of a few can be to the detriment of the 'being' of many others."[21] However, without inflating the sphere of human autonomy, property was recognized as "part of the natural order, which teaches that the individual is prior to society

---

14 Paul VI, *Gaudium et Spes*, § 26.

15 Pius XI, *Quadragesimo Anno*, § 49.

16 Pius XI, *Quadragesimo Anno*, § 114.

17 Pius XI, *Quadragesimo Anno*, § 52; John XXIII, *Mater et Magistra*, § 76.

18 Pius XI, *Quadragesimo Anno*, § 109.

19 Paul VI, *Populorum Progressio*, § 23.

20 John Paul II, *Centesimus Annus*, §§ 6, 30.

21 John Paul II, *Sollicitudo Rei Socialis*, § 31; see also Barrera, *Modern Catholic Social Documents and Political Economy* (Washington, DC: Georgetown University Press, 2001), 218.

and society must be ordered to the good of the individual."[22] For this very reason, concern for the common good also takes priority over any private property rights.[23]

John Paul II upheld private property within limits. In consonance with his emphasis on a personalist ethics, he defined the following priorities: labor takes precedence over capital, and people are more important than things.[24] With this ranking, he confirmed what his predecessors had already taught.[25] John Paul II used the phrase "universal destination of goods" for a principle that Leo XIII had already formulated and that Vatican II had confirmed: that "God intended the earth with everything contained in it for the use of all human beings and peoples."[26] Private property is therefore under a social mortgage, "which means that it has an intrinsically social function."[27] Any individual's right to acquire material goods is legitimately limited by the rights of others to the minimum conditions for a dignified human life. John Paul II concluded "that the possession of material goods is not an absolute right, and that its limits are inscribed in its very nature as a

---

22 John XXIII, *Mater et Magistra*, § 109; see also *Towards a Better Distribution of Land: The Challenge of Agrarian Reform* (Vatican City: Libreria Editrice Vatacana, 1997), §§ 28–31.

23 It was such consideration for the natural law that influenced the German Constitution of 1949, which states: "(1) Property and the right of inheritance shall be guaranteed. Their content and limits shall be defined by the laws. (2) Property entails obligations. Its use shall also serve the public good." (§ 14).

24 See John Paul II, *Laborem Exercens*, § 12.

25 See John XXIII, *Mater et Magistra*, § 106.

26 Second Vatican Council, *Gaudium et Spes*, § 69; John Paul II, *Sollicitudo Rei Socialis*, § 42.

27 Second Vatican Council, *Gaudium et Spes*, § 69; John Paul II, *Sollicitudo Rei Socialis*, § 42.

human right."[28] Because the goods of creation are for the good of all, the reason we own private property is to serve others with it, and therefore our right to property does not extend to hoarding or wasting it. Men are free to acquire property but bound by moral laws in its use and disposal. This holds to an even higher degree for capital goods, on whose good use the livelihood of many may depend.[29]

The universal destination of created goods should not, however, be seen as a license for the state to take over the management of private property. Benedict XVI noted that "we do not need a State which regulates and controls everything, but a State which, in accordance with the principle of subsidiarity, generously acknowledges and supports initiatives arising from the different social forces and combines spontaneity with closeness to those in need."[30] The pope places at the basis of his social teachings the "astonishing experience of gift."[31] We are called to gratuitous giving exactly because we have received as a gratuitous gift from God everything that we believe to be owned by us. Mistaking our property for our own achievements follows from modern man's erroneous belief "that he is the sole author of himself, his life and society."[32] Benedict XVI calls this tendency to assert autonomy a consequence of original sin.

Modern CST on property has developed from a focus on charity to a focus on justice, and recently to a clarification that justice is a means toward "integral human development" for which charity

---

[28] John Paul II, *Centesimus Annus*, § 30; see also the Pontifical Council for Justice and Peace, *Compendium of the Social Doctrine of the Church* (Vatican City: Libreria Editrice Vaticana, 2004), § 177.

[29] John Paul II, *Laborem Exercens*, §§ 14, 18.

[30] Benedict XVI, *Deus Caritas Est*, § 28.

[31] Benedict XVI, *Caritas in Veritate*, § 34.

[32] Benedict XVI, *Caritas in Veritate*, § 34.

serves as the motivator and guide.[33] Social justice does not require socialization of property but imposes a moral and religious duty on the faithful. Catholic social teaching has gone beyond the dichotomy between private and communal property by emphasizing that however property may be held under law it must benefit all. The institution of property as such is a public good.[34] Catholic social teaching has at the same time emphasized the status of all property as a gratuitous gift from God, with a more ambiguous position (pace *Rerum Novarum*) on whether—or, rather, how—it is grounded in natural law.[35] God's sovereignty in any case extends to the works of human hands, which are not created in an autonomous sphere but are brought about under the mandate to Adam "to cultivate the ground from which he was taken" (Gen. 3:23). Because CST regards these issues as decided, it has recently emphasized related concerns of great social importance. Two of these are the destruction of the natural environment and the growing trend toward consumerism.

The universal destination of goods also means that the Creator has given the goods of creation for the ecological well-being of all of creation and not just for the human utility of consumers or producers. There are therefore limits to the appropriation and use of nature. Catholic social teaching opposes reductionist, mechanistic, and utilitarian attitudes toward nature and cautions against the modern tendency to undermine the integrity of the natural world. It also warns of any attempt to attribute a completely independent (and autonomous) existence to man and nature: "A correct understanding of the environment prevents the utilitarian

33 Benedict XVI, *Caritas in Veritate*, § 6.

34 Pontifical Council for Justice and Peace, *Vocation of the Business Leader: A Reflection* (Vatican City: Libreria Editrice Vaticana, 2012), § 36.

35 See Maciej Zieba, *Papal Economics: The Catholic Church on Democratic Capitalism, from* Rerum Novarum *to* Caritas in Veritate (Washington, DC: ISI Books, 2010).

reduction of nature to a mere object to be manipulated and exploited. At the same time, it must not absolutize nature and place it above the dignity of the human person himself."[36] Man and nature have specific roles in the economy of salvation, and man is himself a transcendent part of nature just as humans may up to certain limits change nature. Responsibilities are clearly defined: "The environment is God's gift to everyone, and in our use of it we have a responsibility towards the poor, towards future generations and towards humanity as a whole."[37] The natural environment must not be reserved only to those who can afford to pay for its acquisition or use; it must be preserved in a sustainable manner; and external effects of human behavior must be managed so as to keep crucial common-property resources (such as the atmosphere, oceans, rainforests, and species) intact. Thus, restrictions on private property are justified if they are necessary to fulfill this purpose.[38] As an example of an irresponsible attitude, Benedict XVI mentions the way "some states, power groups and companies hoard non-renewable energy resources," which he says "represents a grave obstacle to development in poor countries."[39] What is required is a "*responsible stewardship over nature*," which is as much a theological and ethical challenge as it is a technological and economic challenge.[40] Stewardship includes the right to use but excludes property in any absolute and exclusive sense.

Consumerism is the (often compulsive) desire to amass movable property through consumption for personal gratification

---

[36] Pontifical Council for Justice and Peace. *Compendium* (Vatican City: Libreria Editrice Vaticana, 2004), § 463.

[37] Benedict XVI, *Caritas in Veritate*, § 48.

[38] See David E. DeCosse, "Beyond Law and Economics: Theological Ethics and the Regulatory Takings Debate," *Boston College Environmental Affairs Law Review* 23 (1996): 829–49.

[39] Benedict XVI, *Caritas in Veritate*, § 49.

[40] Benedict XVI, *Caritas in Veritate*, § 50.

or social status. Locke described approvingly how possessions flow into human self-identity such that having is constitutive of being. This materialist attitude has risen sharply in Western societies and has indeed spread to most of the world. John Paul II and Benedict XVI have repeatedly criticized consumerism.[41] As a "desire to have and to enjoy rather than to be and to grow," frenzied consumption is unworthy of what the human person is called to be.[42] In fact, it is a symptom of spiritual emptiness, which John Paul II (*pace* the Marxist connotations) calls alienation. Placing a greater emphasis on being rather than having—and therefore curtailing desire for property—is always "*a moral and cultural choice*."[43] Benedict XVI clearly states that "*the consumer has a specific social responsibility*" in making choices, despite the influences of marketing and of social pressure.[44] Consumerism is then the self-imposed unwillingness to accept external goods as gifts and to rise above the creature comforts of hedonistic consumption—a refusal to "become more."[45] The antidote to "being selfishly closed in upon himself" (which corresponds to the Augustinian definition of sin) is for man to embrace the model of the Holy Trinity for social relations: mutual gratuitous giving out of charity. Property, then, wants to be shared for achieving human flourishing.[46] By adding advice on how to use property to

---

41 See John Paul II, *Centesimus Annus*, §§ 36, 41, 55, 57; Benedict XVI, *Caritas in Veritate*, §§ 22, 34, 51, 61, 66, 68.

42 John Paul II, *Centesimus Annus*, § 37.

43 John Paul II, *Centesimus Annus*, §§ 41, 36.

44 Benedict XVI, *Caritas in Veritate*, § 66.

45 Benedict XVI, *Caritas in Veritate*, § 14.

46 See Wolfgang Grassl, "*Pluris Valere*: Towards Trinitarian Rationality in Social Life," in *The Whole Breadth of Reason: Rethinking Economics and Politics*, ed. Simona Beretta and Mario Maggioni (Venice: Marcianum Press, 2012).

foster "integral human development," the orientation of recent papal teaching is more pastoral than ever before.

While magisterial CST has been clear on property, as on other issues of social ethics, lay opinion has been more diversified. A wing of liberal (in the classical sense) Catholics, particularly in the United States, emphasizes the creativity, liberty, and responsibility of the individual that is facilitated by private property in democratic and pluralistic societies. They risk overemphasizing human autonomy and neglecting the common good. A wing of conservative Catholics advocates private property but sees its purpose in upholding traditional social values and structures. Following in the footsteps of Bonald, a case in point is the civic movement, Tradition, Family, and Property, that was founded in 1960 by the Brazilian intellectual and Catholic activist Plinio Corrêa de Oliveira and that has spread to other countries: it risks ignoring the value of human freedom. Finally, the various movements of liberation theology, which supported social revolution particularly in Latin America, demanded expropriation through land reform and collectivization. Magisterial CST has officially condemned this school of thought, not least because of its flawed understanding of private property.[47]

The teaching on property of other Christian traditions does not substantially differ from CST. Orthodox doctrine on property is largely in harmony with it. The Russian Orthodox Church explicitly mentions that "the Church does not define property law."[48] Both extremes—contempt for private property and its adulation—are equally shunned and are subordinated to the commandment of love of neighbor. Although the Orthodox Church

---

[47] Congregation for the Doctrine of the Faith, *Instruction on Certain Aspects of the "Theology of Liberation,"* 1984, http://www.vatican.va/roman_curia/congregations/cfaith/documents/rc_con_cfaith_doc_19840806_theology-liberation_en.html.

[48] Église Orthodoxe Russe, *Les fondements de la doctrine sociale* (Paris: Éditions du Cerf—Istina, 2007), 83.

recognizes different forms of property, it does not prefer one over others. Ecclesiastical property, though, must enjoy particular protection because offerings to God are sacred.[49]

With the exception of a few proto-communists (such as the Taborites as the radical wing of the Czech Hussites in the fifteenth century, or the ill-fated rebel leader Thomas Müntzer during the Peasants' War), the Reformers regarded private property rights as part of the order of creation. Luther concentrated on what the law of charity requires, much according to the Pauline exhortation that "those who buy," should act "as though they did not possess" (1 Cor. 7:30). Zwingli was more political and fought against peonage, usury, and monopolies. Some Protestant movements went as far as practicing communal ownership, even more so than did Catholics. The English Diggers, who were dissenters from Anglicanism in the seventeenth century, were agrarian communists. The Plymouth Colony was organized as a form of joint-stock corporation, and the Anabaptist groups of Hutterites in North America continue to practice a near-total community of goods: All property is owned by the colony, and provisions for individual members and their families come from the common resources. The theology of the Reformed tradition has emphasized God's ultimate sovereignty over all creation and goods, which excludes private property as an absolute right. Property rights can only be understood as rights of use or stewardship. The shift in understanding from steward to owner is a defining mark of the fallenness of man.[50] These Protestant interpretations are a far

49 Église Orthodoxe Russe, *Les fondements de la doctrine sociale*, 87.

50 See Murchie, "The New Testament View of Wealth Accumulation"; Amintore Fanfani, *Catholicism, Protestantism, and Capitalism* (Norfolk: HIS Press, 2003), chap. 7; Jon P. Gunnemann, "Capital, Spirit, and Common Wealth," in *The True Wealth of Nations: Catholic Social Thought and Economic Life*, ed. Daniel K. Finn (Oxford: Oxford University Press, 2010), 289–317; R. Scott Rodin, "Stewardship," in *Toward an Evangelical Public Policy*, ed. Ronald J. Sider and Diane Knippers (Grand Rapids: Baker, 2005), 272.

cry from the "Calvinist spirit" as portrayed by Max Weber, which would understand the accumulation of property as an outward sign of God's favor. They are an even farther cry from that caricature of Calvinism that is "prosperity theology" with its promise of personal success and wealth.

VI A Christian View of Property

In its property ethics, Christian thought tries to bring together two statements that at first glance are not easily reconciled. The first statement underscores the importance of private property to freedom and personal development and sees the right to personal property as something natural. The second statement reminds us that God has destined the goods of this earth to benefit all people and nations, and that, therefore, they must also be enjoyed by all. When either statement is divorced from the other, misunderstandings, controversies, or ideologies easily ensue. This holds for Catholic social teaching (CST) as well as for Christian social ethics more generally.

These two truths can be reconciled only if property is not primarily thought of as an economic institution, that is, as one that defines horizontal relations among humans. Rather, it must be understood from within the "anthropological turn" in CST that particularly characterizes the work of John Paul II and Benedict XVI. This approach focuses on the relevance of Christian faith for human life in the here and now and in both its horizontal dimension among humans and its vertical dimension of a relationship with God. Private property is an indispensable means for the human person to root himself and gain a true stake in a community, to secure his future, to express his particular interests and gifts, to make a living for himself and his family, and thus to collaborate with God in the perfection of creation. Like other social institutions, property not only demarcates the reach of persons within society through their ability to consume and produce, it also gives them an opportunity (and for believers imposes on them the duty) to follow Christ in its use. The biblical picture of Jesus as a man of limited means does not imply asceticism as the only way of doing God's will. Christians are not called to mimic Christ's life (which was not one of pure asceticism) in a static and iconic way but to practice, to whatever imperfect degree, the same spirit of charity, compassion, justice, and humility. A Christian view of property must not stop at its economic role; it must also see its transcendent function that helps us become both more human and more Christlike.[1] Property as such is then not at issue; the human attitude toward it is. A proper attitude toward property means seeing it as an instrument for a purpose that transcends private desires while at the same time steering clear of any Pelagian attempt at self-redemption. The crucial point here is whether one can have wealth at all without the accumulation of it, of which Jesus and the apostles clearly warned (Matt. 6:19–21; Luke 12:33–34; James 5:1–6). The just use of property, too, requires grace.

A position on property that aspires to be doctrinally sound and acceptable to a broad cross-section of Christians (although it is particularly committed to the tradition of CST) must be rooted in Scripture, in the teachings of the Church, and in the wisdom of those philosophers and social scientists who sought to understand property not only as a social institution but as a characteristic of human nature. A position in keeping with CST shares little with the (classical or otherwise) liberal tradition even though it, too, advocates private property. The Church has long warned of an

---

1 See Grassl, "*Pluris Valere*: Towards Trinitarian Rationality in Social Life," in *The Whole Breadth of Reason: Rethinking Economics and Politics*, ed. Simona Beretta and Mario Maggioni (Venice: Marcianum Press, 2012).

"idolatry of the market."[2] It teaches that political society is much more than, as liberal thinkers would have it, "a human contrivance for the protection of the individual's property in his person and goods."[3] CST does not support the liberal insistence that private property is a moral absolute that is inextricably linked to the concept of an autonomous self (as is found, for example, in Locke). It is the nature of man as defined by God that legitimizes property and explains its social value and limits.[4] Property rights therefore cannot be derived from the axiom of owning oneself, which is simply opposed to biblical revelation. Property rights are natural but not absolute rights.[5]

The Christian (and particularly the Catholic) view of man is not rooted in individualism and utilitarianism, and it rejects the assumption of human autonomy. If humans are indeed created in God's image and receive everything from him, persons do not have a right over their own lives or those of others (including

---

2 John Paul II, *Centesimus Annus*, § 40.

3 C. B. Macpherson, *The Political Theory of Possessive Individualism: Hobbes to Locke* (Oxford: Oxford University Press, 1962), 264.

4 Free-market economists typically assert the exact opposite, for example, James M. Buchanan, *The Limits of Liberty: Between Anarchy and Leviathan* (Chicago: University of Chicago Press, 1975), chap. 1: "The delineation of property rights is, in effect, the instrument or means through which a 'person' is initially defined." "Persons are defined by the rights which they possess and are acknowledged by others to possess."

5 Claims to the contrary find no foundation in Aquinas nor in recent CST. Yet, there are attempts at reinterpreting CST by undermining the universal destination of goods, for example, in the book *The Church and the Market: A Catholic Defense of the Free Economy*, written by Thomas E. Woods Jr. and published by Lexington Books in 2005, page 194. More genuinely, classical free-market thinkers made no qualms about rejecting Christ's moral teaching, classifying Christian views on property as "extremely destructive," and the Church (both Catholic and Protestant) as an "enemy of society"; see Ludwig von Mises, *Socialism*, trans. J. Kahane (Indianapolis, IN: Liberty Fund, 1981), 378ff.

embryos). Humans are not morally free to decide on just any objective, for goals are ordered by their relative worth. Men are free in the actual pursuit of goals but must abide by the principles of charity and the common good and thus practice responsibility toward others. Contrary to neoliberal (including libertarian) interpretations of Catholicism, which denigrate and sometimes even deride the common good, a truly Catholic view sees the use of property ordered toward it.

Catholic social teaching also repudiates both the conservative and the socialist traditions that deny, for different reasons, the legitimacy of private property, that categorically privilege communal or public ownership, or that see the purpose of property only in supporting social stability. The Church has consistently rejected communism and has opposed expropriation if it did not serve the common good but only another commercial or political interest. Nor should property perpetuate an inherited social order by serving as an exclusion device and thus keeping other social groups from partaking of the "fruit yielding seed" (Gen. 1:29). Property affords people opportunities to serve neighbors, communities, and society. As with other social issues, CST strikes a delicate balance between two extremes and upholds the right to personal property for a social purpose, namely the good of families and other communities. It does not wish to compromise private ownership, though it calls on the state to enforce the social obligations attached to it. The challenge for applying CST lies in balancing the moral goods of private property with the common good.

Property thus raises questions about its purpose, legitimacy, proper acquisition, justified use, and equitable disposal. A viable account must address these by being general yet definite enough to allow for application to specific cases of public interest. A Christian view of property rooted in CST may then be proposed as consisting of the following interrelated propositions:

1. Property has its origin in God and is both a direct and gratuitous gift to individual persons and an indirect concession to humankind through human nature.

   Consequences

   - Human autonomy is nonexistent in the first and at least limited in the second case.
   - Ownership should be understood as good stewardship over entrusted resources.
   - Humans have a duty to give thanks to God for the gifts they have received in either of the two ways.

2. Property is a human right to the extent that it is an ingredient of human nature.

   Consequences

   - Because human rights are given by God rather than by any social compact (such as a constitution), nobody may legitimately abolish property.
   - The right to acquire property is general and does not refer to any specific asset.
   - Property is not a precondition of freedom but rather is its consequence because freedom as part of human nature entails the right to acquire, use, and dispose of property.[6]

3. Property can be held in three forms, which correspond to the three agents of human society—civil society, the market, and the state—and have their own legitimacy and limitations.[7]

---

6 "Private property or some ownership of external goods confers on everyone a sphere wholly necessary for the autonomy of the person and the family, and it should be regarded as an extension of human freedom" (Paul VI, *Gaudium et Spes*, § 71).

7 Benedict XVI, *Caritas in Veritate*, § 37; see also Pontifical Council for Justice and Peace, *Compendium of the Social Doctrine of the Church* (Vatican City: Libreria Editrice Vaticana, 2004), § 180.

Consequences

- Private property is owned by individual persons and is legally both excludable and rival.
- Common property is owned by groups of persons for their collective benefit or that of society at large (e.g., a condominium building).[8]
- State (or public) property is owned by all but administered by public authorities for the benefit of society at large (e.g., national parks or the continental shelf).[9]

4. Property considered private is, properly speaking, personal, where a person is an individual standing in social relations (of kinship, marriage, employment, patronage, gratitude, and so forth) rather than as an abstract bundle of utility functions or rights.[10]

   Consequences

   - Persons have a right to acquire, use, and dispose of property, and this right extends to communities of persons (such as families, firms, associations, cities, and so forth).
   - This right stands under a social "mortgage" whereby property holders have a duty of just acquisition, good use, and equitable disposal.
   - The use of property for purely private purposes, that is, such that produce no good for others, may be sinful.

---

8 The community property of indigenous populations must therefore be respected. See Pontifical Council for Justice and Peace, *Towards a Better Distribution of Land: The Challenge of Agrarian Reform* (Vatican City: Libreria Editrice Vaticana, 1997), § 39.

9 Not everything can be categorized by this tripartite system. There are also things not owned by anyone (*res nullius*), particularly those (such as outer space, sunshine, or most of the seabed) that international law classifies as the "common heritage of mankind."

10 The meaning of *personal property* here has a different emphasis from its use in law where it is movable property as opposed to real property. Real estate can also be personal property in the present sense.

5. Property is not an intrinsic and absolute good but rather a limited and relational good.

   Consequences

   - The Trinity as the model of perfect charity also exemplifies the divine generosity that humans are called to emulate.
   - The use of property should not primarily be seen as a right but as an opportunity for giving.[11]
   - Treating property as an absolute good risks committing the deadly sin of avarice, which can be avoided through practicing the contrary virtue of charity.

6. Property has a social purpose: It is to further the well-being of persons and their communities (families, firms, towns, states, associations, churches).

   Consequences

   - Property presents an opportunity for and means toward producing real human goods; but its purpose also acts as a limit on its use.
   - Distributive effects of property ownership matter and have an ethical relevance.[12]
   - Business leaders are urged to find creative ways to help employees in building property, through employee share ownership plans, profit sharing, or other forms of participation.

7. Property in its three forms is a political institution that requires public protection.

   Consequences

   - There is a duty for lawfully constituted authorities to protect property at two levels: by assuring its inviola-

[11] "The *earthly city* is promoted not merely by relationships of rights and duties, but to an even greater and more fundamental extent by relationships of gratuitousness, mercy and communion" (Benedict XVI, *Caritas in Veritate*), § 6.

[12] Pius XI, *Quadragesimo Anno*, § 57.

bility against incursions by others and by maintaining its social purpose (for example, through just taxation and privileging charitable activities).[13]

- Under the principle of subsidiarity, a broad distribution of property serves to reduce the power of higher-level political authority by giving persons and their communities the means to create meaningful lives independently of state institutions.[14]
- Governments may, under the rule of law, legitimately regulate property rights for specific types of property or specific groups of owners if this is required by the common good.[15]

8. Property is a derived and limited right: It follows from the freedom and dignity of persons and contributes to the satisfaction of their basic needs.[16]

   Consequences

   - Property rights are not absolute because all property ultimately belongs to God; humans are allowed to have property only in accordance with its proper purpose.
   - Under extreme conditions, for instance when the life of others is in danger, property rights can be superseded by higher rights.
   - Seizures of property can only be just if they are required by a public good (and not just any public purpose) and if adequate indemnification is given.

---

13 *Catechism of the Catholic Church*, § 2406.

14 John XXIII, *Mater et Magistra*, §§ 113, 117; Pontifical Council for Justice and Peace, *Towards a Better Distribution of Land* (Vatican City: Libreria Editrice Vaticana, 1997), § 37.

15 Thus, the legal orders of all states have rules on tenancy, labor, taxation, environmental resources, and so forth.

16 *Catechism of the Catholic Church*, § 2402.

9. Property is a right within a hierarchy of rights that require different obligations.[17]

   Consequences

   - In judging these different forms, the effect of property on the well-being of others must be considered.
   - Goods of production (such as land, machines, and practical or artistic skills) oblige owners "to employ them in ways that will benefit the greatest number."[18]
   - Goods of consumption require moderation in use, "reserving the better part for guests, for the sick and the poor."[19]

10. Property ownership poses a moral challenge: to use it justly for virtuous action and to avoid the sinfulness of its wrong use.

    Consequences

    - The use of property reflects the owner's attitude toward God and his personal character.
    - It is incumbent on everyone to respect the goods of other persons including their right to acquire, use, and dispose of property.[20]
    - It is incumbent on the Christian community to encourage its members in their virtuous use of property and correct them in case of any unjust use.

The Catholic view of property as an institution with a divinely ordained purpose deemphasizes the rights of ownership and

---

[17] Different levels of business ownership are distinguished in *Managing as if Faith Mattered: Christian Social Principles in the Modern Organization*, written by Helen J. Alford, OP, and Michael J. Naughton, published University of Notre Dame Press in 2001. See chap. 6.

[18] *Catechism of the Catholic Church*, § 2405.

[19] *Catechism of the Catholic Church*, § 2405.

[20] *Catechism of the Catholic Church*, §§ 2407–2414.

emphasizes the duties associated with it.[21] Particularly in the American experience, "rights talk" risks crowding out full acceptance of the responsibilities that property involves.[22] Abstract property rights do not define social relations. Furthermore, the rights associated with owning a pencil, a dog, a house, and a car may be very different from one another, as they touch upon different types of relations with reality. Even more so, dignity, honor, or freedom may be possessed in yet different ways. Different categories of property will involve specific duties toward God, fellow humans, or animals in one's care. Property rights are thus neither absolute nor uniform nor are their ethical implications.

The liberal tradition, on the contrary, has used a uniform and more abstract concept of property, by associating it with rights rather than purpose. The Catholic (and particularly the Thomistic) understanding of property, of its benefits, and of its social nature is more realistic than Locke's, which still grounds much economic and legal thought. If one indeed had an absolute right over one's body, as Locke suggests, would this not also extend to a fetus in a woman's womb?[23] On the contrary, CST subordinates all forms of life in its various stages to the sovereign ownership of God. Because our bodies, minds, and souls are on loan, we have a duty to give them the best care so as to one day return them to their true owner. Now, the right to private property is closely linked to this duty to contribute to one's personal flourishing, the well-being of one's family, and that of the community as a whole. Having control over more property also involves greater duties toward one's

---

21 Benedict XVI, *Caritas in Veritate*, §§ 7, 43.

22 See Brian J. Benestad, *Church, State, and Society: An Introduction to Catholic Social Doctrine* (Washington, DC: Catholic University of America Press, 2011), 54–58; see also Richard Pipes, *Property and Freedom* (New York: Alfred A. Knopf, 1999), 246.

23 Even on Lockean terms, though, the case is not open and shut, as an argument can be made that the child in the womb is a distinct person who possesses rights and who must be protected from harm.

neighbors. Saint Paul exhorted the "rich in this present world" also to be "to be rich in good works, to be generous and ready to share" (1 Tim. 6:17–18). A good society will give many this opportunity and duty. Private property imposes not only limitations but, maybe even more so, affords opportunities to do good and in so doing to follow Christ (Gal. 6:10). This view of man explains the advocacy, at least since Leo XIII, of broadly distributed ownership, which CST sees as a program for "integral human development."[24] It also accepts that the exercise of legitimate functions of the state (one of which is the protecting of private and public property) also requires taxation. Catholic social teaching has never condemned taxation as theft, beginning with Christ's own example of paying the temple tax (Matt. 17:24–27) and his injunction to pay taxes (Matt. 22:21) and continuing to contemporary teaching that it is unjust not to make social security contributions.[25]

The two extreme approaches to economic policy—laissez-faire capitalism and state ownership—miss the point that what matters is how we treat God and our fellow humans, not merely property relations. Pius XI argued that truly Catholic thought must avoid these "twin rocks of shipwreck."[26] Catholic social teaching offers a middle ground based on human dignity and the common good. Most of all, it reminds us that our relationship to property is not only a matter of political economy but one ruled by personal virtue and responsibility. The Hebrew Wisdom Literature vividly describes that an excess of property may be a bane: "It is a stumbling block to those who are devoted to it, and every fool

[24] See Leo XIII, *Rerum Novarum*, § 65; Pius XI, *Quadragesimo Anno*, §§ 59; John Paul II, *Centesimus Annus*, § 43; Benedict XVI, *Caritas in Veritate*, §§ 4, 8.

[25] *Catechism of the Catholic Church*, § 2436. The term *social security* as used here and in the catechism refers more generally to government safety net programs and not specifically to the American old-age pension system that popularly goes by that name.

[26] Pius XI, *Quadragesimo Anno*, § 46.

will be taken captive by it" (Sir. 31:7 RSV). All the more blessed is he who is affluent and knows how to use his fortune wisely: "His prosperity will be established, and the assembly will relate his acts of charity" (Sir. 31:11 RSV). In St. Luke's parable, what allowed the Good Samaritan to help the half-dead, robbed and abused, victim was the possession of oil and wine, bandage for the wounds, an animal to transport the victim, care at the inn, a prepay of further costs, and the commitment towards future financial responsibility (Luke 10:30–37). This reflects a positive view of property—as an instrument to carry out the command of love for God and neighbor. Property not only facilitates greed but also liberality. But this positive charge of property also requires social encouragement and protection under law. Christian thinking about property, too, must then be guided by the principle that underlies CST: "the proclamation of the truth of Christ's love in society," or "*caritas in veritate in re sociali*."[27] There is a truth about property that must be heeded by people of good will and consists of truths of both faith and reason. What the various sciences can teach us about good stewardship and prudential management falls under the truths of reason, and the divine origin of property and its purpose of advancing the flourishing of human community are truths of faith. Living our lives in accordance with these truths requires charity, as a love of God and neighbor that "rejoices with the truth" (1 Cor. 13:6).

Social science teaches us that three conditions are paramount for the existence of a prosperous civilization: protection of private property ("You shall not steal" and "Thou shalt not covet thy neighbor's house"); honesty and therefore reliability of contracts ("You shall not bear false witness against your neighbor"); and a high esteem for family ("Honor your father and your mother" and "Thou shalt not covet thy neighbor's wife"). Friedrich Engels referred to "three great obstacles" as blocking the path toward

[27] Benedict XVI, *Caritas in Veritate*, § 5.

socialism: "private property, religion, and the present form of wedlock."[28] It is the same conditions that Friedrich von Hayek has identified as indispensable for the existence of free societies, with property at the center.[29] Recognizing what is good for humankind is part of what it means to live truthfully. Only this will make of property what it is meant to be: an expression of both our individuality and our social nature—of what is *proper* to human beings.

---

28 Friedrich Engels, *The Development of Socialism from Utopia to Science*, trans. D. DeLeon (New York: "The People," 1892), 8.

29 See Friedrich A. Hayek, *The Fatal Conceit: The Errors of Socialism* (London: Routledge, 1989), chap. 4.

VII Applications

The value of the Christian view of property sketched above asserts itself when applied to "wicked problems" of public policy.[1] These are characterized by the solution often depending on how the problem is framed or, vice versa, the problem's definition depending on the solution. Such problems are therefore never solved definitively because stakeholders have radically different worldviews and frames of reference for understanding the problem. Some of the public policy issues involving property are of this nature. A Christian perspective rooted in Catholic social teaching (CST) must then break the deadlock between two or more opposing viewpoints claiming equal validity by clearly coming down on one side of the issue and, even more importantly, by showing that a correct framing of the question already implies the only morally defensible answer.

Eminent Domain

Since the formation of states, public authority has claimed the right to seize private property if a substantial public interest in it

---

1 See Horst W. Rittel and Melvin M. Webber, "Dilemmas in a General Theory of Planning," *Policy Sciences* 4 (1973): 155–69.

could be averred.[2] The English common law developed a doctrine of compulsory purchase, which in some jurisdictions became known as eminent domain, by which a sovereign can appropriate private property for reasons of public utility against imdemnification. All land is subject to eminent domain by federal, state, and local governments and is subject to the imposition of taxes, such that there is no true allodial land over which citizens would have sovereignty. The institution derives from the Germanic system of manorial land tenure, under which liege lords retained ultimate sovereignty (*dominium directum*) over a feudal demesne. The Roman law knows no such institution as eminent domain, nor has canon law ever developed any. Civil law jurisdictions with their unitary concept of property are, to the extent that Roman law is still influential, in this regard friendlier toward the protection of private property than are common law jurisdictions.[3]

Eminent domain has provided the justification for numerous seizures by various governments. The Fifth Amendment to the US Constitution allows for such seizures if they are for "public use" under "just compensation." Jurisdiction in the United States holds that the seized property need not actually be used by the public; rather, it must be used or disposed of in such a manner as to benefit the public welfare or public interest. The Supreme Court in 2005 upheld the seizure of private land on behalf of commercial developers in *Kelo v. City of New London*—a 5-4 decision that has remained controversial.[4] The majority opinion found that it was appropriate to defer to the city's decision that

2 See Susan Reynolds, *Before Eminent Domain: Toward a History of Expropriation of Land for the Common Good* (Chapel Hill: University of North Carolina Press, 2010).

3 See Yun-chien Chang and Henry E. Smith, "An Economic Analysis of Civil versus Common Law Property," *Notre Dame Law Review* 88 (forthcoming 2013).

4 545 U.S. 469 (2005), accessed at http://www.law.cornell.edu/supct/html/04-108.ZO.html.

its development plan had a public purpose, saying that "the city has carefully formulated a development plan that it believes will provide appreciable benefits to the community, including, but not limited to, new jobs and increased tax revenue." It later turned out that the developer was unable to obtain financing, that the redevelopment project was abandoned, and that the city did not gain any tax revenue.

Under eminent domain, local governments have repeatedly taken private property for the development of retailers with the argument that a city would benefit from a larger tax base.[5] Entire ethnic neighborhoods have been condemned for building highways, assembly plants, public housing, or "gentrified" urban redevelopment. Family farms have been razed to build power lines. Several states have enacted legislation aimed at reducing the applicability of eminent domain, but the practice continues. An economic case has been made by both sides in the debate. Defenders of eminent domain argue from the greater efficiency of the public use of a formerly private asset and from spillover (or trickle-down) benefits. Opponents object to rent-seeking by private interests that use public authority in an anticompetitive way.[6]

A Christian view of eminent domain and equivalent institutions in other jurisdictions realizes that public goods in the sense of economic theory are not equivalent to the common good as understood by Catholic social ethics. In most cases of public seizing, governments do not even claim to create public goods (such as clean air, street lighting, or national defense). In a society where consumption opportunities abound, an additional supermarket

5 Individual cases of seizures are discussed in *Cornerstone of Liberty: Property Rights in 21st Century America* by Timothy Sandefur and published by the Cato Institute in 2006.

6 See Bruce L. Benson, *Property Rights: Eminent Domain and Regulatory Takings Re-Examined* (New York: Palgrave Macmillan, 2010); Thomas J. Miceli, *The Economic Theory of Eminent Domain: Private Property, Public Use* (Cambridge: Cambridge University Press, 2011).

is merely another private good, and employment or tax revenue created by it hardly justifies the loss of private residences, dislocation of families, and uprooting of social structures. They cannot be understood as contributing to the common good or "integral human development." Social justice will only very rarely require the exercise of the power of eminent domain, although CST has recognized the legitimacy of expropriation in extreme conditions.[7] Catholic social teaching has, however, always given special protection to businesses, including farms on which the livelihood of families depends. Justification of confiscation by the state would therefore have to meet particularly high standards of proof of necessity.[8]

For CST, eminent domain shares only a superficial resemblance with the principle of universal destination of goods, for governments may well intend public use but in most cases simply redistribute goods to other private owners without contributing to the common good. Consequently, resistance against expropriation can, within the limits of the law, be justified even though compensation may be paid.

Intellectual Property Rights

The Church has long taken note of the trend, particularly in advanced economies, toward a dominance of intangibles in the structure of production and consumption: "The possession of know-how, technology, and skill is surpassing land as the decisive factor of production."[9] This raises the question of whether

7 Pius XI, *Quadragesimo Anno*, § 114; Paul VI, *Gaudium et Spes*, § 71; Paul VI, *Populorum Progressio*, § 24.

8 See Pontifical Council for Justice and Peace, *Towards a Better Distribution of Land: The Challenge of Agrarian Reform* (Vatican City: Libreria Editrice Vatacana, 1997), § 38.

9 John XXIII, *Mater et Magistra*, § 106f.; John Paul II, *Centesimus Annus*, § 32.

property means the same in all economic sectors. Can property rights be claimed in the same way over creations of the mind? Should intellectual property rights—copyrights, trademarks, and patents—benefit from the same legal protection that is given to tangible assets? The question is very relevant for CST, which holds that man must regard the goods he possesses "not only as his own but also as common in the sense that they should be able to benefit not only him but also others."[10] Some human inventions such as lifesaving drugs or disease-resistant crops have the potential of doing much good for others subject to their affordability. While private assets such as a house or car hardly generate positive external effects for others, intellectual property can spill over to millions and affect their lives and livelihoods. Catholic social teaching has therefore tended to see it under a social mortgage to an even stronger degree.[11]

Legal trends have gone in the opposite direction by recognizing the possibility of establishing intellectual property rights over ever-larger areas of reality. Rights have expanded in areas ranging from the human genome to the Internet and have been strengthened with legally backed digital fences, lengthened copyright terms, and increased penalties. The U.S. Patent and Trademark Office has issued patents for genes for decades, with such patents currently covering nearly 2,000 human genes and genetic research companies holding patents to about 20 percent of the human genetic code. Not only product but also process inventions have become patentable, including manufacturing techniques, Internet business models, slide-to-unlock features on cell phones, and methods for

10 Paul VI, *Gaudium et Spes*, § 69.

11 See David H. Carey, *The Social Mortgage of Intellectual Property* (Grand Rapids: Acton Institute, 2007); Gabriel J. Michael, "Catholic Thought and Intellectual Property: Learning from the Ethics of Obligation," *Journal of Law and Religion* 25, no. 2 (2009–2010): 415–52.

extracting stem cells from human embryos.[12] Phrases of daily use have been registered as trademarks. Most importantly, common property resources essential for life such as the genetic code have been patented. Biotech companies have established property rights not only over genetically modified crops but also over parts of the human genome sequence. Theoretically, such patents might give corporations the right to charge royalties when couples have a baby if this involves "replicating" a patented gene.[13]

Advocates of intellectual property rights argue that only enforceable protection guarantees the profits that are needed for financing future discoveries and inventions. However, among defenders of free markets, this argument is not unanimously accepted. Critics dispute the necessity of monopolies for fostering innovation, and some advocates of free markets therefore oppose the legal protection of intellectual property rights.[14] Economists point to the high costs of control and enforcement, which essentially amount to an exclusion from using knowledge as a public good.

One argument alleges that patents (and perhaps other intellectual property rights) do not behave like property at all and therefore may not be appropriable. Cross-country evidence shows that whereas the quality of general property rights has a substantial direct effect on economic growth, intellectual property rights

---

12 The Court of Justice of the European Union recently denied the patentability of uses of human embryos for industrial or commercial purposes for violation of morality or *ordre public* (C-34/10 of October 18, 2011).

13 See James Boyle, *The Public Domain: Enclosing the Commons of the Mind* (New Haven: Yale University Press, 2010).

14 See Adam Thierer and Clyde Wayne Crews Jr., eds., *Copy Fights: The Future of Intellectual Property in the Information Age* (Washington, DC: Cato Institute, 2002); Alan G. Isaac and Walter G. Park, "On Intellectual Property Rights: Patents versus Free and Open Development," in *The Elgar Companion to the Economics of Property Rights*, ed. Enrico Colombatto (Cheltenham, UK: Edward Elgar, 2004), 383–413.

have at best only a weak and indirect effect.[15] While the economic nature of patents may be different from land or automobiles, deeper discrepancies at the ontological level have received little attention. Even if it could be shown that patent protection actually reduces innovation, contrary to the claims of its advocates, this argument is a consequentialist one and may garner little credibility for CST.[16] Neither is intellectual property some natural right: it is a deliberately constructed edifice to support invention and innovation.

Indeed, CST has recently questioned whether intellectual property should be regarded like any other type of property. Ideas and innovative capacity are to an even greater extent facilitated by society at large, and they can be a greater boon or bane for social well-being than is other property. Protected monopolies present a barrier to entry and hinder competition. In particular, a restrictive understanding of intellectual property rights excludes the disadvantaged from creative work. The principle of preferential option for the poor calls for skepticism toward a broad construal of such rights.[17] Furthermore, the heavy concentration of intellectual property rights in a small number of highly developed countries runs the risk of perpetuating international inequalities and of putting the preservation of life in poorer countries at peril: "On the part of rich countries there is excessive zeal for protecting knowledge through an unduly rigid assertion of the right to intellectual property, especially in the field of health care."[18] In cases of need, guaranteeing widespread access to life-saving

[15] See Thierer and Crews, eds., *Copy Fights*, chap. 4.

[16] See James Bessen and Michael J. Meurer, *Patent Failure: How Judges, Bureaucrats and Lawyers Put Innovators at Risk* (Princeton, NJ: Princeton University Press, 2008).

[17] See Thomas C. Berg, "Intellectual Property and the Preferential Option for the Poor," *Journal of Catholic Social Thought* 5 (2008): 193–233.

[18] Benedict XVI, *Caritas in Veritate*, § 22.

medication trumps protection of patents, and the violation of intellectual property rights may be justified. A patent holder may be ethically obligated to open access to needed inventions during special emergencies.[19]

From a Christian viewpoint, an important distinction seems to impose itself here. Whereas intellectual property rights over human creations such as films, music, software, or electronic devices are defendable, exclusive rights over parts of nature such as the genome are not. This is not a case of subduing the earth and establishing dominion over it but a misappropriation of God's creation. Naturally occurring biological material, genetic sequences, stem cells, and so forth can no more be patented validly than can one legitimately establish property over another person. Catholic social teaching has therefore unequivocally condemned all attempts to define life as an invention instead of a freely given gift of God. John Paul II repeatedly addressed the issue and welcomed genetic research but repudiated attempts at appropriating forms of life for commercial purposes.[20] Treating the essential components of life as tradable assets involves a deterministic and reductionist view of the human person. This is an issue on which leaders of many faith communities are agreed, which has led to common positions on genetic engineering.[21]

---

19 International trade law and national statutes allow for compulsory licenses for both patents and copyrights.

20 John Paul II, Address to the Pontifical Academy of Sciences, October 28, 1994, published in *Osservatore Romano* (English edition), no. 45 (November 9, 1994), 3. See also Pontifical Council for Justice and Peace, *Compendium of the Social Doctrine of the Church* (Vatican City: Libreria Editrice Vaticana, 2004), §§ 472–480.

21 See Keith D. Warner, "Are Life Patents Ethical? Conflict between Catholic Social Teaching and Agricultural Biotechnology's Patent Regime," *Journal of Agricultural and Environmental Ethics* 14, no. 3 (2001): 301–19; Marilyn Martone, "The Ethics of the Economics of Patenting the Human Genome," *Journal of Business Ethics* 17, no. 15 (1998): 1679–84.

The monopoly that patent holders have over lifesaving drugs is another case in point. In 2001, the US Congress and President George W. Bush seriously considered "breaking" the patent that Bayer AG holds on Cipro in order to stockpile the drug in the face of a potential anthrax attack. Under pressure, the German pharmaceutical company agreed to a long-term contract with the US government at an unusually low price.[22] Because no lives were actually in danger and the government simply wanted to prepare for a potential threat, and because no just compensation was paid, CST would likely not accept this politically motivated strong-arming as a just taking of an intellectual property right.

In March 2012, the Indian government granted its first compulsory license ever to Indian generic drug manufacturer Natco Pharma Ltd. for Sorafenib tosylate, a cancer drug patented by Bayer under the brand name Nexavar. The ruling was justified by small exports to India at unaffordable prices for many cancer patients.[23]

The application of CST to this case is not unambiguous. Although Natco has to pay Bayer royalties at the maximum rate allowed by international trade law, which may be understood as just compensation, the contribution of the decision to the common good is debatable. The Indian government could have negotiated for a higher import volume of the drug and offered subsidies to patients who need it instead of creating a windfall for a domestic generic drug manufacturer. When infringing property rights, subsidiarity requires using the least drastic measure to

---

22 See Michael, "Catholic Thought"; Dennis D. Crouch, "Nil: The Value of Patents in a Major Crisis Such as an Influenza Pandemic," *Seton Hall Law Review* 39, no. 4 (2009): 1125–36.

23 Geeta Anand and Rumman Ahmed, "Bayer Gets Setback in India," *Wall Street Journal* (March 13, 2012), B2.

achieve the desired outcome.[24] It is undisputed that "it is a strict duty of justice and truth not to allow fundamental human needs to remain unsatisfied, and not to allow those burdened by such needs to perish."[25] The Church has therefore repeatedly urged better access to generic drugs particularly in poorer countries, and Benedict XVI has reaffirmed this desire.[26] Yet CST has also consistently considered whether a seemingly easy solution does not perhaps create more harm than it does good and, therefore, whether alternatives exist to achieve the same or a better result at lower economic and social costs. Ultimately, holding a patent over a drug that is badly needed in an area where affordability is low does require action—charitable action by its owner and regulatory action by government should all other options fail.

Business Ownership

Economists tend to view a firm as a bundle of property rights or as assets owned by stockholders. According to the corporate governance model of the United States, a corporation is a thing and can therefore be owned (even though the legal fiction of a "nexus of contracts" may be used). The shareholders are the owners, and the primary duty of those who manage a firm is then to maximize the interests of its shareholders in dividends or a higher company value.

Diverse legal forms of business have developed that differ by ownership, capital structure, and control. Corporations must be distinguished from sole proprietorships, partnerships, cooperatives, and others depending on legal forms available in various jurisdictions. Particularly, corporations are governed by the pri-

[24] See Frank Pasquale, "Joining or Changing the Conversation? Catholic Social Thought and Intellectual Property," *Cardozo Arts & Entertainment Law Journal* 29, no. 3 (2011), 681–727, especially 686–702.

[25] John Paul II, *Centesimus Annus*, § 34.

[26] Berg, "Intellectual Property," *Journal of Catholic Social Thought*, 197f.

mary (or even exclusive) purpose of maximizing profits. In the United States, and to a smaller extent in other capitalist economies, corporations have also experienced an increasing separation between ownership and control.[27] The easy transferability of shares on stock markets and household investment in equities for the purpose of savings has given the reins of corporations to a powerful managerial class. Yet corporate power remains highly concentrated rather than diffused.[28] Managers are often exposed to the pressure of only a few institutional stockholder groups, and their decisions are largely guided by financial markets, especially by the opportunity of bonus payments and the threat of external takeover. Thus, shares have become a very different type of property from, say, furniture, automobiles, or real estate. While these are "active" property, shares are merely "passive" property.[29] For the vast number of shareholders, equity does not come with rights other than to receive a dividend if such is paid out. This has created principal-agent problems, that is, misalignments between the incentives of shareholders with those of managers. But agency conflicts are different from how they have often been envisaged. Given concentrated ownership, the relevant conflict is actually between large shareholders and managers or between large shareholders and small shareholders.

An equally worrying trend has been the financialization of the economy, particularly in the United States, with financial markets dominating over the "productive" economy and trade. Mergers and acquisitions became more promising strategies than

---

[27] The classic work propounding this argument is Adolf A. Berle and Gardiner C. Means, *The Modern Corporation and Private Property* (New York: Macmillan, 1932).

[28] See Clifford G. Holderness, "The Myth of Diffuse Ownership in the United States," *Review of Financial Studies* 22, no. 4 (2009): 1377–1408.

[29] See Berle and Means, *The Modern Corporation*, bk. 4, sec. 3.

the cumbersome process of developing new products.[30] In combination, the two trends have given rise to a business sector where management largely unchecked by owners of capital pursues maximization of profits through financial maneuvers rather than contributes to the common good of satisfying consumer needs and wants.

Catholic social teaching has never supported the property-rights view of firms that is an ingredient of free-market economics. In particular, it has indicted publicly held limited liability companies and corporations for their reduced accountability:[31]

> The laws passed to promote corporate business, while dividing and limiting the risk of business, have given occasion to the most sordid license. For We observe that consciences are little affected by this reduced obligation of accountability; that furthermore, by hiding under the shelter of a joint name, the worst of injustices and frauds are perpetrated.

This view of corporate activity is one of the reasons why Benedict XVI advocates that civil society impresses the values of solidarity and gratuitousness on corporations so as to "civilize the economy" and make a contribution to the true human good.[32] Considering a business only as a financial or legal entity—as a "society of capital goods"[33]—is overly reductionist.

Contrary to US law, CST does not see a firm as a thing but as a social entity, particularly a community of persons engaged in common work and sustained by relationships to the firm's social,

---

30 This is not to say, of course, that such financial activities do not ever serve a legitimate purpose, only that their predominance raises dangers from the perspective of CST.

31 Pius XI, *Quadragesimo Anno*, § 132.

32 Benedict XVI, *Caritas in Veritate*, § 38.

33 John Paul II, *Centesimus Annus*, § 43.

political, economic, and natural environment.[34] John Paul II taught that "the purpose of a business firm is not simply to make a profit, but is to be found in its very existence as a *community of persons* who in various ways are endeavouring to satisfy their basic needs, and who form a particular group at the service of the whole of society."[35] Shareholders and managers are then not free to make decisions according either to their own interests or even those of the firm as an isolated entity. They are morally (and in some countries legally) bound to balance such considerations with interests of other stakeholders. Catholic social teaching has long recognized principal-agent problems "between the ownership of productive goods and the responsibility of company managers."[36] Benedict XVI explicitly endorses a reorientation, because "business management cannot concern itself only with the interests of the proprietors, but must also assume responsibility for all the other stakeholders who contribute to the life of the business."[37]

Catholic social teaching sees the responsibility of companies go beyond that typically assumed in the business ethics literature.[38] It is not exclusively negative, such as the duty to not overtly harm customers, employees, or the natural environment; a firm must obviously ensure that it never undermines the dignity of all who

---

34 See Helen J. Alford, OP and Michael J. Naughton, *Managing as if Faith Mattered: Christian Social Principles in the Modern Organization* (Notre Dame, IN: University of Notre Dame Press, 2001), chaps. 2 and 6; Lloyd E. Sandelands, *God and Mammon* (Lanham, MD: University Press of America, 2010), chap. 5.

35 John Paul II, *Centesimus Annus*, § 35.

36 John XXIII, *Mater et Magistra*, § 104.

37 Benedict XVI, *Caritas in Veritate*, § 40.

38 Susan J. Stabile, "A Catholic Vision of the Corporation," *Seattle Journal for Social Justice* 4, no. 1 (2005): 181–202.

are affected by its economic activities.[39] This alone imposes specific moral limitations; for example, abstention from the use of a business for the production or dissemination of pornography.[40] There are also positive responsibilities, particularly the development of products that are truly good and services that truly serve,[41] the implantation of numerous family businesses, the re-equilibration of the economy by reducing the financial sector to its proper purpose of facilitating consumption and investment, and the creation of a corporate governance system that protects the investment of smaller shareholders while also defining a just commitment to other stakeholder groups.

For CST, then, corporate ownership implies special responsibilities because capital is a type of property that comes with a special social mortgage. It creates new wealth through the productive use of resources, particularly of persons with their skills, knowledge, and diligence, but it must also serve them and their communities well for it to be properly used. Every firm has a duty to promote, rather than to detract from, the common good.[42] Business creates a great number of such goods, and the augmentation of personal property is one of them.[43] It can make "an irreplaceable contribution to the material and even the spiritual well-being of humankind."[44] More concretely, particularly in the United States, the population at large must find ways to build up property that

---

[39] *Catechism of the Catholic Church*, § 2405; Pontifical Council for Justice and Peace, *Vocation of the Business Leader: A Reflection* (Vatican City: Libreria Editrice Vaticana, 2012), § 30.

[40] *Catechism of the Catholic Church*, § 2354.

[41] See *Vocation of the Business Leader*, §§ 9, 40, 42.

[42] See George E. Garvey, "The Theory of the Firm, Managerial Responsibility, and Catholic Social Teaching," *Journal of Markets and Morality* 6, no. 2 (2003): 525–40; Sandelands, *God and Mammon*, chap. 7.

[43] See Robert G. Kennedy, *The Good That Business Does* (Grand Rapids: Acton Institute, 2006), chap. 5.

[44] *Vocation of the Business Leader*, § 2.

goes beyond investing in stocks, bonds, or mutual funds, and this can only be expected by reinvigorating business ownership. Private property in means of production can all the more contribute to two goals at the heart of CST—strengthening families by creating economic opportunities for others.

References

Church Documents

All documents issued by Roman authorities can be found on the website of the Holy See under the respective pontificates or institutions of the Curia at http://www.vatican.va. The most important documents that make pronouncements on property are the following:

Encyclicals and Constitutions

Leo XIII. *Rerum Novarum* (1891).

Pius X. *Singulari quadam* (1912).

Pius XI. *Quadragesimo Anno* (1931).

John XXIII. *Mater et Magistra* (1961).

Second Vatican Council. *Gaudium et Spes* (1965)

Paul VI. *Populorum Progressio* (1967).

John Paul II. *Laborem Exercens* (1981); *Sollicitudo Rei Socialis* (1987); *Centesimus Annus* (1991).

Benedict XVI. *Deus Caritas Est* (2005); *Caritas in Veritate* (2009).

Other Documents

Catechism of the Catholic Church. Vatican City: Libreria Editrice Vaticana, 1997.

Code of Canon Law (*Codex iuris canonici*), 1983.

Pontifical Council for Justice and Peace. *Towards a Better Distribution of Land: The Challenge of Agrarian Reform.* Vatican City: Libreria Editrice Vaticana, 1997.

Pontifical Council for Justice and Peace. *Compendium of the Social Doctrine of the Church.* Vatican City: Libreria Editrice Vaticana, 2004.

Pontifical Council for Justice and Peace. *Vocation of the Business Leader: A Reflection.* Vatican City: Libreria Editrice Vaticana, 2012.

Secondary Literature

Alford, Helen J., OP, and Michael J. Naughton. *Managing as if Faith Mattered: Christian Social Principles in the Modern Organization.* Notre Dame, IN: University of Notre Dame Press, 2001.

Almodovar, António, and Pedro Teixeira. "The Ascent and Decline of Catholic Economic Thought, 1830–1950s." *History of Political Economy* 40 (2008).

Avila, Charles. *Ownership: Early Christian Teaching.* Maryknoll: Orbis Books, 1983.

Barrera, Albino, OP. *Modern Catholic Social Documents and Political Economy.* Washington, DC: Georgetown University Press, 2001.

Becker, Lawrence C. *Property Rights: Philosophic Foundations.* London: Routledge, 1977.

Benestad, J. Brian. *Church, State, and Society: An Introduction to Catholic Social Doctrine.* Washington, DC: Catholic University of America Press.

Benson, Bruce L. *Property Rights: Eminent Domain and Regulatory Takings Re-Examined.* New York: Palgrave MacMillan, 2010.

Berg, Thomas C. "Intellectual Property and the Preferential Option for the Poor," *Journal of Catholic Social Thought* 5 (2008).

Berle, Adolf A., and Gardiner C. Means. *The Modern Corporation and Private Property.* 1932. Reprint, New York: Harcourt, Brace & World, 1968.

Berlin, Isaiah. "Two Concepts of Liberty." In *Four Essays on Liberty*. London: Oxford University Press, 1969.

Berman, Harold J. *Law and Revolution: The Formation of the Western Legal Tradition*. Cambridge: Harvard University Press, 1983.

Bessen, James, and Michael J. Meurer. *Patent Failure: How Judges, Bureaucrats and Lawyers Put Innovators at Risk*. Princeton, NJ: Princeton University Press, 2008.

Boyle, James. *The Public Domain: Enclosing the Commons of the Mind*. New Haven: Yale University Press, 2010.

Brague, Rémi. *Eccentric Culture: A Theory of Western Civilization*. South Bend, IN: St. Augustine's Press, 2002.

Brown, Donald. *Human Universals*. Philadelphia: Temple University Press, 1991

Brundage, James A. *Medieval Canon Law*. London and New York: Longman, 1995.

Buchanan, James M. "Property as a Guarantor of Liberty." In *Property Rights and the Limits of Democracy*. Edited by Charles K. Rowley. Cambridge: Cambridge University Press, 1993.

Buchanan, James M. *The Limits of Liberty: Between Anarchy and Leviathan*. Chicago: University of Chicago Press, 1975.

Buckle, Stephen. *Natural Law and the Theory of Property: Grotius to Hume*. Oxford: Clarendon Press, 1991.

Carey, David H. *The Social Mortgage of Intellectual Property*. Grand Rapids: Acton Institute, 2007.

Chang, Yun-chien, and Henry E. Smith. "An Economic Analysis of Civil versus Common Law Property." *Notre Dame Law Review* 88 (2013).

Coase, Ronald H. "The Problem of Social Cost." *Journal of Law and Economics* 3 (1960).

Colombatto, Enrico, ed. *The Elgar Companion to the Economics of Property Rights*. Cheltenham, UK: Edward Elgar, 2004.

Cortés, Juan Donoso. *Esseys on Catholicism, Liberalism, and Socialism.* Translated by W. McDonald. Dublin: M. H. Gill, 1879.

Coughlin, John J., OFM. *Canon Law: A Comparative Study with Anglo-American Legal Theory.* Oxford: Oxford University Press, 2011.

Crouch, Dennis D. "Nil: The Value of Patents in a Major Crisis Such as an Influenza Pandemic." *Seton Hall Law Review* 39, no. 4 (2009).

Cuccia, Tiaiana, and Walter Santagata. "Collective Property Rights for Economic Development: The Case of the Ceramics Cultural District in Caltagirone, Sicily." In *The Elgar Companion to the Economics of Property Rights.* Edited by Enrico Colombatto. Cheltenham, UK: Edward Elgar, 2004.

De Soto, Hernando. *The Mystery of Capital.* New York: Basic Boods, 2003.

DeCosse, David, E. "Beyond Law and Economics: Theological Ethics and the Regulatory Takings Debate." *Boston College Environmental Arrairs Law Review* 23 (1996).

Demsetz, Harold. "Toward a Theory of Property Rights." *American Economic Review* 57, no. 2 (1967).

Dougherty, Richard J. "Catholicism and the Economy: Augustine and Aquinas on Property Ownership." *Journal of Markets & Morality* 6, no. 2 (2003).

Fanfani, Amintore. *Catholicism, Protestantism, and Capitalism.* Norfolk: HIS Press, 2003.

Franks, Christopher A. *He Became Poor: The Poverty of Christ and Aquinas' Economic Teachings.* Grand Rapids: Eerdmans, 2009.

Friedman, Milton, and Rose Freiedman. *Free to Choose.* San Diego: Harcourt, 1980.

Garvey, George E. "The Theory of the Firm, Managerial Responsibility, and Catholic Social Teaching." *Journal of Markets and Morality* 6, no. 2 (2003).

Grabill, Stephen J. "Protestant Social Thought." *Journal of Markets & Morality* 12, no. 1 (2009).

Grassl, Wolfgang, and Andre Habisch. "Ethics and Economics: Towards a New Humanistic Synthesis for Business." *Journal of Business Ethics* 99, no. 1 (2011).

Grassl, Wolfgang. "Hybrid Forms of Business: The Logic of Gift in the Commercial World." *Journal of Business Ethics* 100, suppl. 1 (2011).

Grassl, Wolfgang. "*Pluris Valere*: Towards Trinitarian Rationality in Social Life." In *The Whole Breadth of Reason: Rethinking Economics and Politics*. Edited by Simona Beretta and Mario Maggioni. Venice: Marcianum Press, 2012.

Gunnemann, Jon P. "Capital, Spirit, and Common Wealth." In *The True Wealth of Nations: Catholic Social Thought and Economic Life*. Edited by Daniel K. Finn. Oxford: Oxford University Press, 2010.

Habel, Norman C. *The Land Is Mine: Six Biblical Land Ideologies*. Minneapolis: Fortress Press, 1995.

Habiger, Matthew, OSB. *Papal Teaching on Private Property: 1891–1981*. Lanham, MD: University Press of America, 1990.

Hardin, Garrett J. "The Tragedy of the Commons." *Science* 162, no. 3859 (1968).

Hayek, Friedrich A. *The Fatal Conceit: The Errors of Socialism*. London: Routledge, 1989.

Holderness, Clifford G. "The Myth of Diffuse Ownership in the United States." *Review of Financial Studies* 22, no. 4 (2009).

Isaac, Alan G., and Wlater G. Park. "On Intellectual Property Rights: Patents versus Free and Open Development." In *The Elgar Companion to the Economics of Property Rights*. Edited by Enrico Colombatto. Cheltenham, UK: Edward Elgar, 2004.

Kennedy, Robert G. *The Good That Business Does*. Grand Rapids: Acton Institute, 2006.

Landes, William M., and Richard A. Posner. *The Economic Structure of Intellectual Property Law*. Cambridge, MA: Belknap Press, 2003.

Liggio, Leonard P., and Alejandro A. Chafuen, "Cultural and Religious Foundations of Private Property." In *The Elgar Companion to the*

Economics of Property Rights. Edited by Enrico Colombatto. Cheltenham, UK: Edward Elgar, 2004.

Macpherson, C. B. *The Political Theory of Possessive Individualism: Hobbes to Locke*. Oxford: Oxford University Press, 1962.

Martone, Marilyn. "The Ethics of the Economics of Patenting the Human Genome." *Journal of Business Ethics* 17, no. 15 (1998).

Meidinger, Errol. "Property Law for Development Policy and Institutional Theory: Problems of Structure, Choice, and Change." In *The Mystery of Capitol and the Construction of Social Reality*. Edited by Barry Smith, David M. Mark, and Isaac Ehrlich. Chicago: Open Court, 2008.

Miceli, Thomas J. *The Economic Theory of Eminent Domain: Private Property, Public Use*. Cambridge: Cambridge University Press, 2011.

Michael, Gabriel J. "Catholic Thought and Intellectual Property: Learning from the Ethics of Oblication." *Journal of Law and Religion* 25, no. 2 (2009–2010).

Miller, Robert T. "The Coase Theorem and the Preferential Option for the Poor." *Journal of Catholic Social Thought* 5 (2008).

Mises, Ludwig von. *Human Action*. 4th ed. San Francisco: Fox & Wilkes, 1996.

Mises, Ludwig von. *Socialism*. Translated by J. Kahane. Indianapolis, IN: Liberty Fund, 1981.

Munzer, Stephen R. *A Theory of Property*. Cambridge: Cambridge University Press, 1990.

Murchie, David. "The New Testament View of Wealth Accumulation." *Journal of the Evangelical Theological Society* 21, no. 4 (1978).

Nell-Breuning, Oswald von, SJ. *Reorganization of Social Economy*. New York: Bruce Publishing Company, 1936.

Nell-Breuning, Oswald von, SJ. "The Formation of Private Property in the Hands of Workers." In *The Social Market Economy: Theory and Ethics of the Economic Order*. Edited by Peter Koslowski. Berlin: Springer, 1998.

Nemo, Philippe. *What Is the West?* Translated by K. Casler. Pittsburgh: Duquesne University Press, 2006.

Nisbet, Robert. *The Social Philosophers: Community and Conflict in Western Thought*. New York: Thomas Y. Crowell, 1973.

Novak, Michael. *The Spirit of Democratic Capitalism*. New York: Simon & Schuster, 1982.

Nozick, Robert. *Anarchy, State and Utopia*. New York: Basic Books, 1974.

Pesch, Heinrich, SJ. *Ethics and the National Economy*. Translated by Rupert Ederer. Norfolk: HIS Press, 2004.

Pettit, Philip. "Freedom in the Market." *Politics, Philosophy and Economics* 5, no. 2 (2006).

Pipes, Richard: *Property and Freedom*. New York: Alfred A. Knopf, 1999.

Pleins, J. David. *The Social Visions of the Hebrew Bible: A Theological Introduction*. Louisville: Westminster John Knox Press, 2000.

Reynolds, Susan. *Before Eminent Domain: Toward a History of Expropriation of Land for the Common Good*. Chapel Hill: University of North Carolina Press, 2010.

Rittel, Horst W., and Melvin M. Webber, "Dilemmas in a General Theory of Planning." *Policy Sciences* 4 (1973).

Rodin, R. Scott. "Stewardship." In *Toward an Evangelical Public Policy*. Edited by Ronald J. Sider and Diane Knippers. Grand Rapids: Baker, 2005.

Russe, Église Orthodoxe. *Les fondements de la doctrine sociale*. Paris: Éditions du Cerf—Istina, 2007.

Sandefur, Timothy. *Cornerstone of Liberty: Property Rights in 21st Century America*. Washington, DC: Cato Institute, 2006.

Sandelands, Lloyd E., *God and Mammon* (Lanham, MD: University Press of America, 2010.

Schumpeter, Joseph A. *History of Economic Analysis*. New York: Oxford University Press, 1954.

Siegan, Bernard H. *Property and Freedon: The Constitution, the Courts, and Land-Use Regulation*. Piscataway, NJ: Transaction Publishers, 1997.

Spieker, Manfred. "The Universal Destination of Goods: The Ethics of Property in the Theory of a Christian Society." *Journal of Markets & Morality* 8, no. 2 (2005): 333–54.

Stabile, Susan J. "A Catholic Vision of the Corporation." *Seattle Journal for Social Justice* 4, no. 1 (2005).

Stuckenschmidt, Heiner, Erik Stubkjaer, and Christoph Schlieder, eds. *The Ontology and Modelling of Real Estate Transactions*. Aldershot: Ashgate, 2003.

Swift, Louis J. "*Iustitia* and *Ius Privatum*: Ambrose on Private Property." *American Journal of Philology* 100, no. 1 (1979).

Thierer, Adam, and Clyde Wayne Crews Jr., eds. *Copy Fights: The Future of Intellectual Property in the Information Age*. Washington, DC: Cato Institute, 2002.

Todd, Walker F. *Progress and Property Rights: From the Greeks to Magna Carta to the Constitution*. American Institute for Economic Research, 2009.

Tully, James. *A Discourse on Property: John Locke and His Adversaries*. Cambridge: Cambridge University Press, 1980.

Viner, Jacob. *Religious Thought and Economic Society*. Edited by J. Melitz and D. Winch. Durham: Duke University Press, 1978.

Warner, Keith D. "Are Life Patents Ethical? Conflict between Catholic Social Teaching and Agricultural Biotechnology's Patent Regime." *Journal of Agricultural and Environmental Ethics* 14, no. 3 (2001).

Weimer, David L. "The Political Economy of Property Rights." In *The Political Economy of Property Rights*. Cambridge: Cambridge University Press, 1997.

Woods, Thomas E., Jr. *The Church and the Market: A Catholic Defense of the Free Economy*. Lanham, MD: Lexington Books, 2005.

Zieba, Maciej. *Papal Economics: The Catholic Church on Democratic Capitalism, from* Rerum Novarum *to* Caritas in Veritate. Washington, DC: ISI Books, 2010.

About the Author

Wolfgang Grassl is a full professor of business administration and holds the Dale and Ruth Michels Endowed Chair in Business at Saint Norbert College (De Pere, Wisconsin). He has degrees in philosophy and economics and after a career in business and public policy in Austria has taught and pursued research at universities and colleges in several countries including Hillsdale College (Michigan), University of the West Indies (Jamaica), Open University (UK), University of Innsbruck (Austria), and Oxford University (UK). He is the author or editor of five books and of more than one hundred articles and reviews in the fields of business studies, economics, philosophy, and intellectual history that have recently appeared in periodicals such as the *Journal of Business Strategy*, the *Journal of Business Ethics*, the *Journal of Management Development*, the *Catholic Social Science Review*, the *History of Economic Ideas*, the *Journal of Entrepreneurship Perspectives*, and the *Analecta Praemonstratensia*. His research focuses on consumer behavior, marketing strategy, business ontology, Catholic social thought, and the history of the Premonstratensian Order.

17029185R00060

Made in the USA
Middletown, DE
02 December 2018